Using your overhead projector and other visual aids

Using your overhead projector and other visual aids

Chris Waller

FORDIGRAPH
Division of Ofrex Ltd.
London

Published by the Fordigraph Division
of Ofrex Ltd.
Ofrex House, Stephen Street, London.
W1A 1EA.

First published 1983.

ISBN 0 86221 016 X

This book is based on the visual aids
training workshops devised and arranged
by Christine Waller who retains the
copyright of this material in such a form.

Photoset by
Rowland Phototypesetting
Bury St Edmunds, Suffolk
Printed in England by
W. S. Cowell Ltd.
Butter Market, Ipswich

Produced by The Archon Press Ltd.

Designed by Robert Hillier
of David Cook and Associates
and illustrated by
Pat Bennet and Joan Hickson

Acknowledgements

My thanks to
David Watson for listening so patiently while I talked through my ideas.
And to Ray Klarnett of Gordon Audio Visual for his advice on the Diazo
Section.

Contents

Introduction

The book

The purpose of this book is to provide a step-by-step guide to the production and use of visual aids. It covers the basic principles of effective visual communication, including such problem areas as:

- Presenting statistics
- Ad-libbing with aids
- What to do if you can't draw

The book is entirely practical in its approach to visual aids. It deals with the 'hows' and 'whys' of production and presentation rather than the 'whys' and 'wherefores' of visual aids and the communication and learning process.

It is intended to be a do-it-yourself manual, and what I write is drawn from direct experience as a producer and user of visual aids and from the feedback received from those who have attended my visual aids training workshops.

The contents are based on my workshop training programme, the techniques for which have been successfully tried and tested by UK as well as overseas trainers, teachers, managers, secretaries and sales representatives among others, who have often had no previous knowledge of visual aids production methods.

This is a visual book

One point frequently brought to my attention is the difficulty of presenting text in a brief but visually interesting way while not losing its meaning. Not all information lends itself to illustration by a suitable picture or cartoon, nor does the user always have time to think one up.

To provide you with some ideas, I have included a variety of diagrams and charts which summarize the important points in the accompanying text. There are also the explanatory drawings to help you through the process of production and presentation.

The jargon

As with all specialist subjects, visual aids have their own language. It is tedious to have to keep referring to a glossary, so I have given a brief explanation (often in brackets) after each term as it is used. Where necessary, I have gone into further detail in a relevant section of the book. So please read on; you will always find a full answer where it is most apt.

The characters

To simplify matters, this is my generalization:

The Presenter or Speaker is the person who conveys the information.
The Audience are those who watch and listen.

The cartoon figure is Bill; he is my assistant and your guide. At times he can be good for a laugh, and when I am short of ideas I am sometimes tempted to use him as a filler. But there is always the danger that you may start to pay more attention to Bill than to me! You will find more about 'distractors' on pages 91–94.

How to use this book

You will not need to have read this book from start to finish before you can begin to make use of it. The contents page lists the chapter headings, and at the end of each chapter there is a visual summary or review of the contents so that what you need can be found at a glance. To section the book in this way, I have sometimes had to repeat information.

As you read, think of the text as the verbal part of a lesson or lecture, with the illustrations and summaries as the supporting visual aids. This will show you how I have used simple pictures which are easy to understand and remember to explain or emphasize the main points.

What are visual aids?

'Aids to communication, learning, teaching, remembering and research which utilize the sense of sight' *The Glossary of Training Terms

The term visual aid is used to describe both the equipment and the visuals.

This book deals with those aids which are in general use:

- The overhead projector
- Whiteboards
- Flip charts

I have omitted the blackboard since it does not require sophisticated visual materials and the basic requirements such as letter heights, are the same as those for the whiteboards.

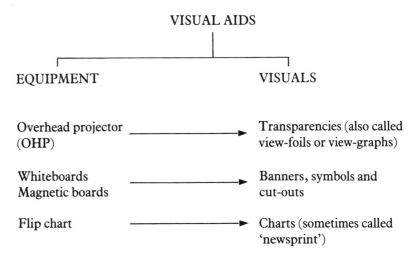

NB Visual aids are only seen, but audio visual aids are seen and heard (CCTV, tape-slide projectors, films with sound).

The visuals, either pictures, diagrams, symbols or written words, contain the information that is displayed and seen while the presenter talks. They can be used to attract attention and to reinforce or visually explain selected parts of a lesson, seminar or other verbal presentation. The TV weatherman's map and the railway or airline announcement screens are visual aids which help to convey their particular messages as quickly and easily as possible. Try to imagine troughs and depressions over the North Sea with snow in Wigan and rain in South Wales. Those pictures and symbols are not used only for their entertainment value.

Why use visual aids?
To improve communication between speaker and audience.

Research has shown that up to 30 per cent more comprehension and 40 per cent more retention are possible when multi-sensory (using several senses) channels of communication are used correctly.

At the beginning I promised not to theorize. I shall simply and briefly show the benefits to be derived from the correct use of visual aids – other than the advantage of **seeing** and **hearing** the information **simultaneously**.

IMPROVED COMMUNICATION

EQUIPMENT
- Easy to use
- Used in normal light conditions and positioned at front – speaker maintains eye-to-eye contact with audience and can adjust the presentation according to their reaction

VISUALS
- Attract attention
- Describe – places, people, products, situations, etc.
- Explain – complicated points
- Reinforce – important points
- Summarize – main points

VISUAL DISPLAY TECHNIQUES
Allow presenter to
- Pace rate at which information is displayed
- Build up complex information step-by-step
- Animate static pictures

Visual comment Flow charts are a simple way to separate information and are visually more interesting than lists. Such a diagram could be shown a section at a time by using the appropriate display technique; see page 61.

Who can use visual aids?

Anyone who has to give a speech, inform or instruct others, sell an idea, service or product, or in any way communicate with a group of other people can use visual aids to support the chat.

They are widely used in industry, commerce and education. The equipment is easy to set up and use. The visual materials are simple to produce without having to spend a lot of time or money, and although professionally produced visuals are available, many speakers (or their secretaries/assistants) prefer to make their own.

Like most things, it is a matter of practice. As one avid user I know remarked, 'To work without my aids would be like putting a Frenchman in a straitjacket.'

1. The equipment

- OVERHEAD PROJECTOR (OHP) (page 5)
- WHITEBOARDS – Wet wipe (pages 71, 72, 75, 76)
  - Dry wipe (pages 71, 72, 75, 76)
  - Magnetic (pages 71, 72, 77–80)
- FLIP CHARTS (newsprint) (pages 71–74)

Visual aids provide an effective, efficient medium for putting across ideas and information in a way that is simple and easy to follow. They are particularly useful when a personal approach is called for. All the equipment is used in normal daylight or artificial light conditions and is positioned at the front of the room.

The speaker faces the audience throughout. This enables him or her to maintain 'eye-to-eye' contact with the group, assess their reaction and, if necessary, adjust the presentation. The audience can also ask questions and raise points as and when they occur. Thus each session can be geared to the individual needs of each group.

A visual summary of this section might be shown by the accompanying illustration.

```
VISUAL AIDS FOR IMPROVED COMMUNICATION

  • INSTANT FEEDBACK
  • INSTANT FLEXIBILITY
```

Introducing the overhead projector

The **overhead projector** provides a means of quickly conveying visual information to a large audience or small group of people without breaking the personal link between speaker and audience.

Unlike most other types of projector, the OHP can be used in normal light conditions without the quality of the projected image being impaired. It is positioned at the front of the room alongside the presenter who uses the aid to show the visual materials which are needed to reinforce, summarize or explain selected parts of the chat.

The presenter controls the rate at which the visual information is displayed, and can adjust the pace or visual content to suit the needs of each group. (See further, ad-libbing with aids, page 81.)

The machine is simple to operate, and the **visuals** (transparencies) are easy to produce; they can be prepared in advance and used many times, so saving the presenter the bother of repeatedly chalking up the same diagrams, as he would have to do if he was using a blackboard.

The OHP is also a boon for those who cannot draw since there are several ways of producing professional-looking transparencies without needing to have any artistic expertise whatsoever; see pages 35–42.

The overhead projector (OHP)

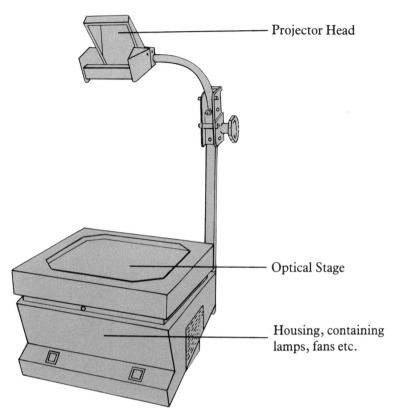

Projector Head

Optical Stage

Housing, containing lamps, fans etc.

The OHP projects large 250 mm×250 mm (10″×10″), 250 mm× 200 mm (10″×8″), A4 transparencies and transparent and translucent objects such as perspex models. With careful preparation, simple science experiments can also be displayed to a larger audience than might otherwise be possible.

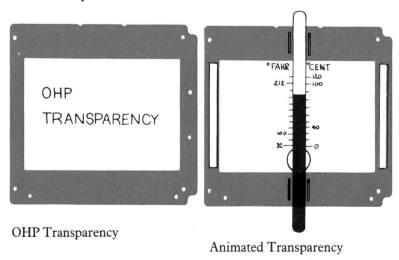

OHP Transparency

Animated Transparency

Types of OHP

There are a variety of OHPs on the market, ranging from the sturdy 'childproof' machines found in schools, to those with 35-mm attachments for showing slides as well as transparencies, and lightweight models that fold down into their own carrying cases. All OHPs are portable, but you may prefer to use one of the special trolleys for moving machines from room to room.

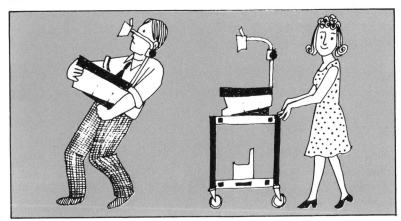

ALLOW THE OHP TO COOL DOWN BEFORE MOVING IT OR YOU MAY DAMAGE THE LAMP.

Transparencies can be prepared in advance or during the presentation if the speaker needs to ad lib. The impromptu notes and diagrams can be put on to sheets of film or on the roll of film that winds across the projector stage. (Transparency production starts on page 17.)

The film roll can be wound across the projector stage to provide a 'blackboard' facility for OHP users.

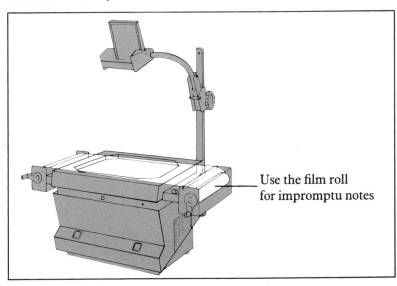

Use the film roll for impromptu notes

It is not a good idea to draw a complete presentation on to the roll because:
- It is difficult to use the visuals out of sequence.
- It is almost impossible to decide where to leave the blanks for the impromptu notes.
- Other speakers may remove your markings to make room for their own.

Apart from that, it is a waste of time and a distraction for the audience if you have to clean the roll as you talk; just use a water-soluble OHP pen or OHP pencil and remove the markings with a damp cloth at the end of the session, leaving the film clear for the next presenter.

Screens

Screens are not essential as the OHP will project a reasonable image on to any smooth, light surface. A better reproduction is, however, obtained when a screen is used.

The best screen for OHP work has a matt white finish, and this reflects light over a wider area than does a directional screen. Whiteboards can also be used instead of screens (see pages 75 and 89).

Screen fabrics can be mounted on board and this helps to eliminate any variations in focus caused by wrinkles on the surface and makes the screen easier to angle correctly.

Roller screens stand on their own tripods and are portable.

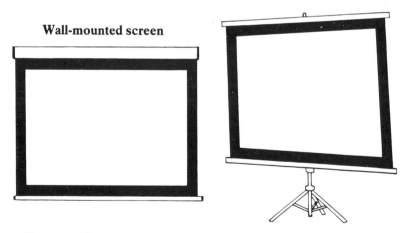

Wall-mounted screen

To ensure that everyone has an unobstructed view:
- Raise screen to 1.75 metres (about 5 or 6 feet) above the floor level.
- Presenters stand clear of the screen (or sit down).

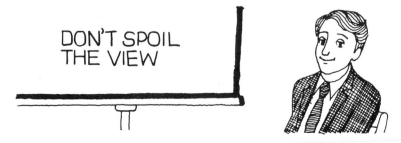

DON'T SPOIL THE VIEW

Projected image size

This can range between 1.4 and 2.2 square metres (5 and 8 square feet), depending on the focal length of the projector's objective lens and the distance between the projector and the screen. The closer the OHP is to the screen, the smaller the picture will be.

Wide-angle, shorter focal-length projectors can be placed closer to the screen, which makes them ideal for use where space is limited. It is reasonable to assume that the easier it is for the audience to see, the more likely they are to keep looking. Therefore project as large a picture as possible.

Setting the projector

Projectors vary in construction and the position of lamps and switches, so it is impossible to give precise instructions. Nevertheless, here is the general procedure:

1. Plug in and arrange lead so that nobody can trip over it – especially the presenter.
2. Dust OHP stage with anti-static cloth or soft, lint-free cloth.
3. Switch on fan and lamp – these switches may be separate or combined.
4. Adjust picture size by carefully moving OHP closer to (smaller) or further from (larger) the screen.
5. Focus so that there is a crisp, black outline around the projected area – and then check this by projecting your own special 'test' transparency, which should contain fine linework and very small lettering and so is quite unsuitable for normal use.

Focusing the OHP

Do this by simply raising or lowering the projector head on the column. The further the OHP is from the screen, the lower the head will need to be.

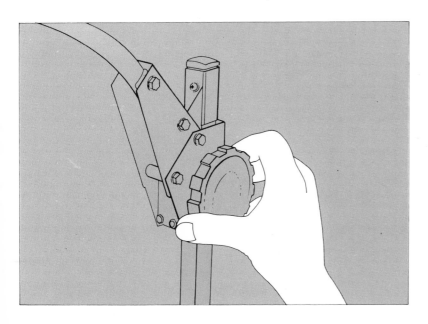

The ideal picture shape is symmetrical, either square or oblong depending on shape of projector stage.

- To obtain this, align the projector head and screen so that they are parallel and the axis of the light beam hits the screen at 90°.

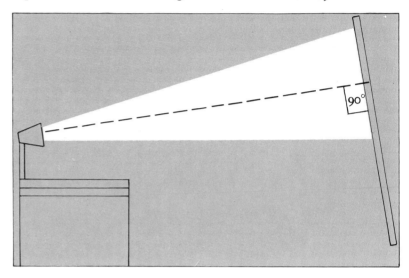

Working in less than ideal conditions

Sometimes it may be necessary to throw the picture high up on to the screen so that everyone can see easily. Under such circumstances, simply do the best you can because the resulting 'keystone' effect is not in itself a problem unless you are dealing with geometric or other precise shapes which may be distorted by a less than perfect reproduction.

Sometimes 'keystoning' causes the edge of a transparency to be slightly out of focus, but this can usually be overcome by keeping the picture within a certain area; see pages 11, 25.

Rooms with low ceilings

The height of the room itself may prevent you from projecting the picture well above the audience's heads, making it difficult for the back row to see the information on the bottom of the screen. If you know beforehand that you will be up against this problem, put the important facts in the top half of the visual (see page 25) and remember to give the remainder of the information verbally.

Keeping your OHP in working order

The overhead projector is a reliable machine which rarely needs major repairs unless it is mistreated. Maintenance is mostly a matter of cleaning lenses and replacing lamps.

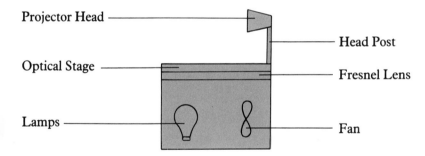

Projector Head
Optical Stage
Lamps
Head Post
Fresnel Lens
Fan

Anything you feel unsure about can be left to a technician, but neither of you will ever be faced with a problem like this –

Visual comment. Cartoons or 'funnies' as I call them can enliven a dry topic, but be careful: they must be relevant and if you use too many they'll lose their impact and act as distractors, see pages 91–94.

Lenses

Projector head outside lenses. When necessary, dust with anti-static or lint-free cloth or clean using OHP lens cleaner or mild detergent solution.

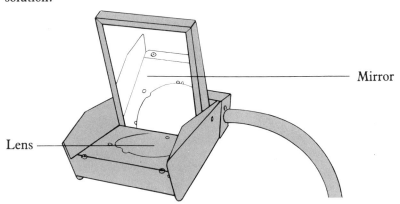

Fresnel (condenser) lens. The Fresnel (named after its inventor, Augustin-Jean Fresnel, 1788-1827) or condenser lens is the most expensive part of an OHP and can be damaged by:

- HEAT – On older projectors, leave fan running throughout presentation to cool lens. Modern projectors are thermostatically controlled.
- ABRASIVES – Avoid using abrasive cleaners (even paper towels can scratch this lens).
- DUST – Cover OHP with plastic cover to protect from dust.
- SPIRIT – Do not use spirit to clean an acrylic lens.

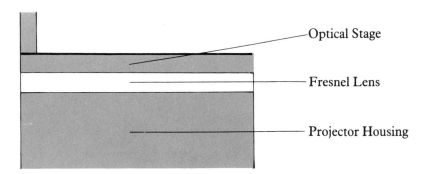

In some machines, the Fresnel lens and optical stage are hermetically sealed to prevent dust from collecting on the lens surface. In this case only the outside surfaces will require occasional cleaning. If the dust is not removed from the optical stage and Fresnel lens it will, eventually, dim the projected image.

Cleaning the Fresnel lens:
- Use a soft lint-free cloth and OHP lens cleaner or mild detergent solution. Work in a circular motion, following the direction of the lens.

Cleaning the optical stage:
- Dust with anti-static or lint-free cloth before use.
- Occasionally clean, using lens cleaner or mild detergent solution.

*TAKE CARE NOT TO SCRATCH THE LENSES AS ANY
MARKS MAY PROJECT PERMANENTLY.*

The lamp
OHP lamps vary considerably in price and the cost of replacement is worth considering when you buy a projector. Replacing low-cost lamps can more than offset the extra cost of an initially more expensive model.

Changing the lamp. This is as easy as changing a domestic light bulb so long as you remember:
- To keep spare available
- To allow OHP to cool first – this is to protect the lamp, not your fingers.
- Not to touch lamp with bare hands
- To follow manufacturer's instructions – they are simple, but they vary.

Secondary lamps. Some OHPs contain a secondary lamp which can be switched into position and immediately take over from the first. Before relying on this, **check**:
- The secondary lamp is working and in place.

How to make sure that everyone can see
It is important to ensure that everyone has an unobstructed view of the screen and that the presenter can work in comfort.

Placing the people. These seating plans ensure that everyone has a clear view of the screen without having to move.

Sometimes it is not possible to rearrange the fixtures and fittings, but if you check the viewing area beforehand you should be able to discourage the audience from sitting where the visibility is poor or restricted.

If you plan to use more than one aid, make sure that the speaker can move easily and quickly between pieces of equipment.

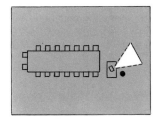

Centre Arrangement

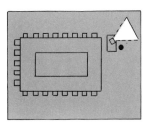

Corner Arrangement

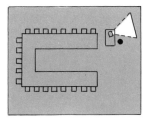

Horseshoe Arrangement

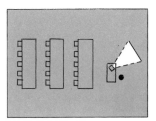

Classroom Arrangement

Placing the screen. The screen needs to be higher than the audience's heads, between 1.5 and 1.8 metres (5 and 6 feet) above floor level.

If the light is reflected off the screen at an angle, it will make some parts of the room unsuitable for viewing. This can be overcome by angling the screen as shown in the seating plans.

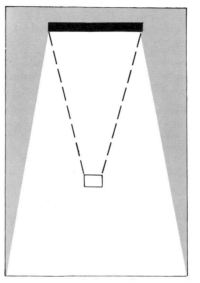 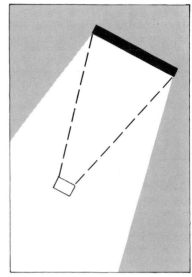

Shaded area is unsuitable for viewing.

Placing the presenter. Obviously the presenter will be up front, with easy access to the aids. Although he or she may need to be as much 'on show' as the visuals themselves, it is essential for the speaker not to block the view. Whether the speaker sits or stands is a matter of personal preference. In an informal situation, I usually sit to put my audience at ease, but if I am addressing a large audience, I stand, making sure that I am out of the way of the aids.

Presentation techniques are covered on pages 95–98.

Using the OHP correctly

In general, overhead projectors in any one institution will be used by several people, and unless there is a technician to set up and check the equipment, it is often left to the individual user to discover whether or not the aid is working properly.

If this is your problem, try to arrive before the audience so that you have a chance to align and focus the projector and check the seating arrangements. Quite apart from the professional aspect of a well-prepared and presented programme, there are other benefits to be gained from this:

- EXTRA PRESENTATION TIME – the beginning of the session is not wasted checking or changing equipment.
- EQUIPMENT REMAINS IN BACKGROUND – the 'limelight' belongs to the presenter and the visuals. If the audience's attention becomes focused on how you communicate rather than what you're communicating, it will be a distractor; see pages 91–94 for other distractors.

Visual comment. This time, I have set out the checklist under **do's** and **don'ts** to make it easy to follow and remember. Here, first, are the **do's**.

Do make sure		If not
• OHP PLUGGED IN AND WORKING	→	Check plug, change lamp/projector.
• PROJECTED IMAGE IS BRIGHT	→	Clean the lenses, see page 12.
• PROJECTED IMAGE IN FOCUS	→	See page 9.
• VISIBILITY IS GOOD	→	Check from back row, enlarge picture by moving OHP further from screen.
• SUFFICIENT SPACE ON FILM ROLL	→	Clean or change the roll.
REMEMBER TO:		
• LEAVE FAN RUNNING THROUGHOUT	→	This is to cool the Fresnel lens.
• TURN OFF LAMP BETWEEN VISUALS	→	To bring audience's attention back on to yourself. A brilliant, blank screen acts as a distractor.

The correct procedure is:
TURN ON projector
TALK ON subject
TURN OFF projector

DON'T

- LOOK AT THE SCREEN – Remember, you focused before you started and the transparency is the right way up on the projector for you to read it.
- POINT TO THE SCREEN – Apart from losing the eye-to-eye contact with the audience, you could damage the screen. Point on the transparency. (You can use a pencil or one of the special OHP pointers.)
- STARE OR FIX YOUR GAZE ON ONE SECTION OF THE AUDIENCE – Keep your eyes moving to make everyone feel that you are talking to them personally. And to assess their reaction. Presentation techniques are covered on pages 95–98.

Summary of overhead projector benefits

- Easy to use.
- Simple to maintain.
- Ideal for personal communication.
- *Presenter* – remains in control throughout.
  - can ad lib or adjust presentation to suit each group.
- *Software* – transparencies easy to produce.
  - no drawing abilities required; see page 35.

And, for the final visual, here is a mnemonic checklist to remind you of the main points:

Check
LAMP – spare/working.
EQUIPMENT – clean/working.
ANGLES – screen, projector head, position of screen in room.
ROOM LAYOUT – can they all see easily? And remember:

> *VIEWING IS EASIER WHEN PRESENTERS KEEP OUT OF THE WAY*

2. A B C of good visuals

Visual aids differ from other forms of visual communication such as books, posters and printed advertisements because they are as a rule seen for only a limited time and therefore cannot be studied in depth or read at the viewer's leisure.

A good visual contains only the essential information: the key points or hooks on to which the details can be hung.

Simple visuals are easier to read, remember and take notes from. If the visual information needs to be detailed, then break it down into its component parts and present it in easy to digest stages; see pages 61, 74, 80.

LIMIT YOURSELF TO ONE IDEA PER VISUAL

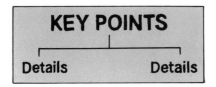

Be accurate

This seems an obvious statement to make, but one can unintentionally mislead or confuse the audience, so watch out for those hidden distractors, such as:

- MISSPELLINGS
- INACCURATE FACTS – Make sure the visual information corresponds with the verbal and update visuals when necessary.
- EMPHASIS ON UNIMPORTANT POINTS – this usually happens because colour is wrongly used or lettering sizes are inconsistent.

Be brief

Visuals that are used to reinforce, explain or summarize the spoken word should be kept simple and to the point so that the contents can be quickly read and assimilated and the information retained for as long as possible.

If necessary, the speaker can add further visual information while speaking to the audience, see 'Ad Libbing with Aids', pages 81–82.

As results from tests show, approximately 40 to 50 words are the maximum that can be easily absorbed in one go. Therefore try to keep within that limit. You can always use another visual or provide printed handouts.

Be
Restrained
Include only
Essential
Facts

Visual comment. Succinct memory-jogger (another mnemonic).

Be clear

This can be divided into two sections: the **contents** and the **graphics**. The graphics section starts on page 22.

The contents

Do not Confuse the audience with

      Language they do not understand

      Explain technicalities and

      Ambiguous information.

      Resist the temptation to embellish the visual with a maze of details that sidetrack the viewers or draw their attention away from the

      MAIN POINT

It can be tempting to use an existing visual because it is attractive, readily available or simply the one your predecessor always worked with, and, of course, you can always adapt the chat to suit the pictures . . .

Be careful. The visuals must be completely relevant for them to convey their message to the audience. It is pointless if the presenter is describing the tractor in the bottom left-hand corner while the audience is fascinated by the flock of geese flying across the middle of the screen.

This could lessen their comprehension of the entire subject, not only of that particular visual. (More about distractors on page 91.)

Selecting the information

Producing good visuals is not just a matter of artistic expertise. The objective is to convey your message as quickly as possible, without leaving any doubts in the audience's minds as to precisely what you mean.

A simple transparency or chart which achieves this is preferable to a visual masterpiece which does not, but if you can manage both, the resulting presentation should be well worth watching.

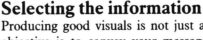

IF TIME IS LIMITED, SPEND IT ON THE PREPARATORY WORK— SIMPLIFYING THE CONTENTS SHOULD CUT PRODUCTION TIME ANYWAY

The procedure

There are various ways of tackling this, and I find the following method simple and successful.

1. Read script or lecture notes, select and mark points needing visual reinforcement, explanation, etc.
2. When designing a complete presentation, include an introduction and summaries.
   The format is the same as for any type of instruction –
   'Tell 'em what you'll tell 'em'   – **Introduction**
   'Tell 'em'   – **Content**
   'Tell 'em what you told 'em'   – **Summary**
3. Decide whether to use words or pictures (or both) for each visual; varying the types of visual can help to hold the audience's attention.
4. Try to limit the visual information to the key points. Too much visual information (especially if it is all on one transparency) can be confusing. Only include what the audience must or should know and omit what it would be nice for them to know.
   a. Précis text.
   b. Keep illustrations bold and simple.
   c. Do not include any points that you will not discuss.
5. Select points to be emphasized.
6. Decide whether to use display techniques and separate information for these.
7. Produce.

Summary

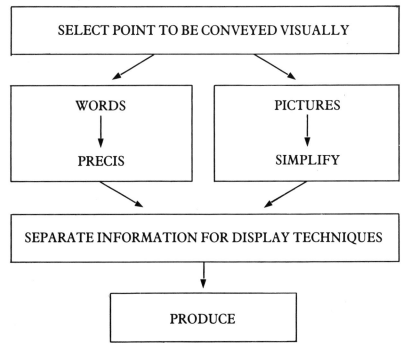

Getting someone else to produce the visuals

This is a good idea if you are short of time or need professional artwork to impress an important client. However, the graphic requirements for visual aids are different from many other forms of visual communication and it is as well to make sure that the producer is aware of the following points.

CONSTRAINTS	POINTS TO WATCH		REFER PAGE
Viewing distance from back row to screen.	READABILITY	Lettering Linework	28 26
Daylight viewing (no blackout)	VISUAL IMPACT	Use of colour	43
Limited viewing time	SIMPLICITY	One idea at a time, or use display techniques	61, 74, 80

The producer will also need to know *exactly*:
- What to include or exclude if working from detailed drawings or notes.
- What to emphasize.
- Where to break complex information for display techniques.
- When you need the visuals.

Allow time to check or amend if necessary, and even if you are lucky enough to have an artist or MRO on the premises, remember that they may have other work to do or that the job you are giving them to do may not be as simple as it looks.

SO ALLOW SUFFICIENT TIME AND MAKE YOUR INSTRUCTIONS CLEAR

3. Software production

A GOOD VISUAL IS:
- Big and Bold
- Clear and Concise
- Stimulates Interest
- Attracts Attention
- GETS THE MESSAGE ACROSS

Overhead projector

Although this section is primarily concerned with transparency-making techniques, some of the ideas can be applied to the other visual aids.

For easy reference, I have put the production and graphics requirements for whiteboards and flip charts into separate chapters.

OHP transparency production procedure

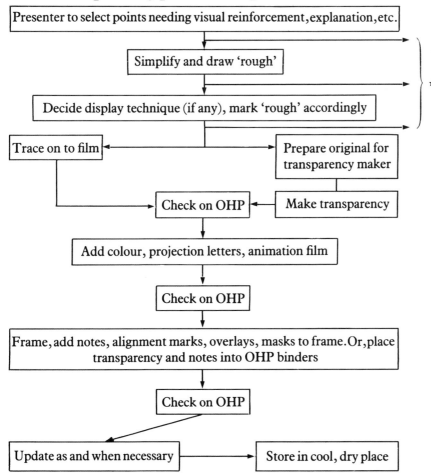

*The information can be passed on for production at any one of these stages, depending on the ability of the producer.

Which OHP pen to use

- Water-soluble (non-permanent)   • Spirit-based (permanent)

OHP pens contain a fast-drying ink which does not bead (bubble) on film. They are available in a range of projectible colours and several line widths:

Fine ——————— For detail work
Medium ——— Ideal for hand-lettering, outlines, etc.
Broad ■■■■ For thick lettering, outlines, etc.

Always recap immediately after use to stop the tips from drying out.

Water-soluble pens and markers are easily erased with a damp cloth and should be used for impromptu notes or work which will not be needed again.

OHP pencils are water-soluble and will not dry out if the cap is left off.

Spirit-based pens and markers need a special solvent or OHP eraser to remove them from film, so use these pens for work that you want to keep.

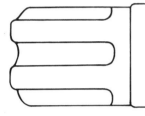

ALWAYS REPLACE CAP IMMEDIATELY AFTER USE TO STOP THE TIPS FROM DRYING OUT

Overhead projector graphics

Visual aids do not need to be works of art, but it helps if they are visually pleasing. So let's take a look at ways of achieving this, even if you cannot draw.

Contents –
- Drawing a 'rough' plan
- Layout and linework
- Lettering
- So what if you can't draw
- Use of colour
- Reprographics
- Framing, storing and updating
- Display techniques and animation

Drawing a 'rough' plan

Whether the visual consists of words, pictures or a combination of the two, in the long run it is faster to draw a 'rough' plan first.

Advantages
- The contents can be easily altered.
- Information can be marked up for overlays, masks, etc.
- Points needing emphasis can be selected and marked.
- Overall visual effect can be considered and adjusted if necessary.
- The 'rough' plan can be shown to another person for comment, approval or production.

The procedure

Equipment needed – Transparency frame (size according to OHP stage)
Pencils
6 mm (¼-inch) squared paper (use non-reproducible blue or red for thermal copying)

1. Place the transparency frame on the paper and draw around the inside to mark the overall projection area. OHP projector stages vary in size, so make sure that the frame fits or is smaller than the stage otherwise the visual will be too big and the projected picture will be incomplete.

2. Mark 12 mm (½-inch) inside the frame area to avoid the distortion that can occur on some projectors.

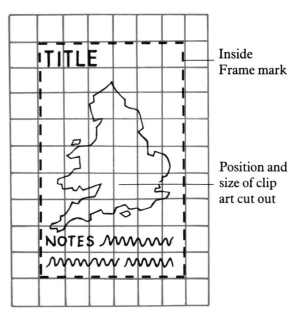

The transparency can be landscape or portrait

3. Using the squares as lettering and drawing guides, plan a rough layout of the visual, including the title, captions and diagrams, and position and size of clip-art cut-outs. Then transfer the rough to a suitable base for projection or reproduction.
   a. Trace on to film to obtain a direct copy or for Diazo copying.
   b. Trace on to thin paper for Thermal copying, or ink directly over the top of the non-reproducible base.
   c. Trace on to thin paper for plain paper copying.
   For reprographics, see pages 47–58.

Some OHP frames have a press-out centre ruled with squares. Use this for the rough, tape film in place and trace, press out the centre, and the transparency will be ready for use.

The centre can then be used as cutting board.

Layout and overall design

- The layout needs to be balanced and tidy with the information grouped logically.
- Words and pictures should be as large as possible to make sure that they are easily visible.
- Try to use the entire projection area without overcrowding or adding details just for the sake of filling the space.
- Limit your ideas to one per visual or use one of the display techniques described on page 61 to separate the information.
- Highlight important points by placing them just above centre – this is the point of maximum visual impact.

> *MASK OFF UNUSED, SURROUNDING AREA*
> *TO DRAW EYES ON TO MESSAGE*

Colour film or a blackout mask can be used to eliminate the surrounding area.

Blackout masks are made from paper and mounted in the frame with the transparency.
1. Mark the area outline on the rough plan.
2. Using a sharp blade and straight edge, cut out the shape carefully.
3. Mount the mask in the frame with the transparency.
If you want to keep the rough, use a paper copy for masking.

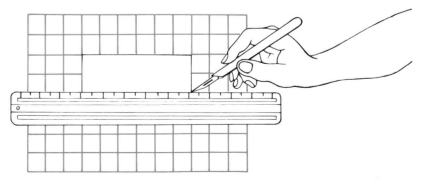

Basic layout for normal projection. Place the picture or diagram in the centre with the title at the top and notes on either side; notes should be aligned horizontally and vertically.

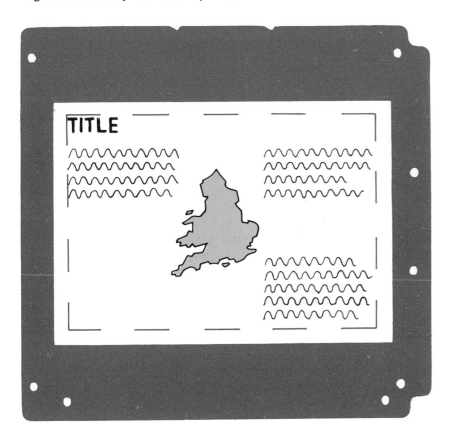

Layout for low projection. Put the important information in the top half of the visual so that those at the back will be able to see it.

Aligning notes and text. It is not necessary to centre lines of text since this takes time. In any case, unless it is accurate it will look untidy. It is simpler to align the notes and blocks of text from the left-hand side.

Titles are not absolutely essential, but are helpful to the audience and are best placed in the top left-hand corner.

> # Centring text takes time and looks untidy unless it is accurate.

Linework

Linework should be **bold** ▬▬▬ 1.5 mm (1/16th″) wide and limited simple outlines and essential information.

Faint lines can disappear when projected, and lines too close together often merge. So keep the drawings basic and to the point. Not only will the visual result be better, but production time will be cut.

The left hand illustration has more visual impact

You don't need a drawing board. Use squared paper for guidelines and a straight edge to rule along.

The rough can be drawn directly on to this paper, or a thin sheet of paper can be placed over the top and the lines beneath used as a guide for drawing and lettering.

There are special pads of film with a squared guide sheet, and these can be used rather like a writing pad.

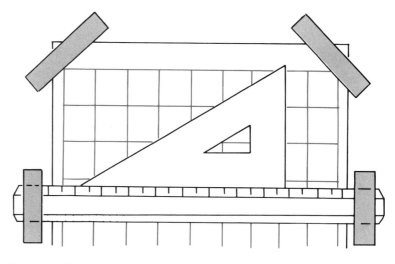

General rules

1. Use **bold** lines, approximately 1.5 mm (1/16th″) wide.
2. Keep a uniform line width. Avoid a mixture of thick and thin.
3. Avoid shading. Cross hatch / / / / / / / or apply colour (see page 43).
4. Do not mix grades of pencil. Use 2B for thermal copying.

Lettering

Lettering must be legible and easy and quick to read from the back row of the audience.

The contents should be brief and to the point.

A copy of a typed handout does not make an effective visual; the lettering may be difficult or even impossible to read. If you have no alternative or no time to do anything else, look at page 85, but ideally, the visual should be CLEAR and CONCISE, LIMITED TO THE KEY POINTS.

Lettering guidelines

1. 40 to 50 words maximum per visual.
2. 6 mm (¼-inch) high CAPITALS minimum.
3. Lower case (small letters) easier to recognize.
4. Capitals for titles or emphasis.
5. Line space for legibility.
6. Emphasize important points.
7. Use uniform letter size for points of equal importance.

A) Unimportant Point

b) important point

Visual comment: A has more visual impact than b, it is a distractor.

Number of words per visual. It has been found that 40 to 50 words can be easily absorbed from one visual. The lettering guide contains forty words and still manages to say a lot.

USE 40/50 WORDS MAX, ALIGN FROM LEFT,
KEEP IT LEGIBLE AND CHECK SPELLING.

Actual letter size – unprojected. 6 mm (¼-inch) high capitals are adequate for the average-size training room, but, in a lecture hall, letter heights need to be proportionally larger to ensure readability from the back row. This is a point to watch if you intend writing on the film during the presentation.

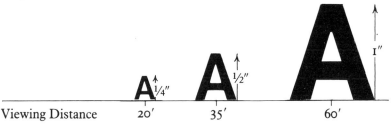

| Viewing Distance | 20′ | 35′ | 60′ |

NB. The size of the accompanying lower case (small letters) will be slightly less than the capitals.

Letter style. Lower-case letters are easier to recognize *en masse* than are capitals. They have a more distinct shape, and since most of what we read is printed in lower case, it is also a matter of familiarity. So try to use small letters for the main part of the text and capitals for titles and emphasis.

However, if you are hand-lettering and find block capitals easier, use those rather than illegible lower case.

Highlighting information. Important points can be emphasized by:
Altering *Style*
       Colour
       SIZE
       Underlining
       Or by adding the information while presenting; see page 82.

Line spacing for legibility. Lines too closely spaced are difficult to read, so leave at least the height of the capital letters between the lines, and preferably more if space allows.

Blocks of information can be visually separated by leaving extra space between each section.

Letter spacing will have to be assessed 'by eye', unless you are using a typewriter or lettering machine.

A general guide for OHP is to leave slightly more space around each letter than if you were printing on to paper.

T H I S   I S   T O O   O P E N

THIS IS TOO CLOSE

THIS IS JUST RIGHT

Types of lettering for use on visuals

- Handlettering
- Stencilling
- Dry transfer letters
- Typewriting and lettering machines

Handlettering

Handlettering can be visually interesting and pleasant to look at, but it must be **bold** and **legible**. If your handwriting is not up to scratch, PRINT carefully, using the squares on the 'rough' to help to keep the letters to a consistent size and evenly spaced.

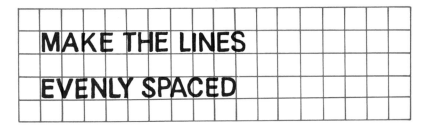

MAKE THE LINES

EVENLY SPACED

Another way to keep lettering straight is to print along a rule or straight edge.

KEEP LETTERING STRAIGHT

USING A STRAIGHT EDGE

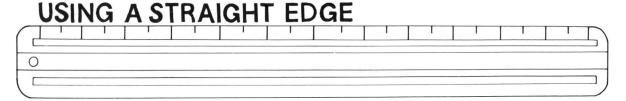

Lettering on the film roll can be a problem, but you can obtain ruled acetate sheets which can be slipped under the roll to provide the guidelines.

Stencilling

Stencilling is a fast, simple way in which to provide tidy lettering. Stencils are available in a variety of styles, the open typefaces being more suitable than those which are condensed.

If you do not have a drawing board and tee square, use a squared guide sheet, a straight edge and sticky tape. See p.26.

You can stencil on to paper using a technical drawing pen or special stencil nib, or work directly on to film using an OHP ordinary pen or OHP technical pen. Make sure the ordinary pen fits the stencil; they are not custom-made for the job.

Plastic drawing inks can be used on AV film, but will take longer to dry than the special OHP inks. For details of the inks, turn to pages 22, 40.

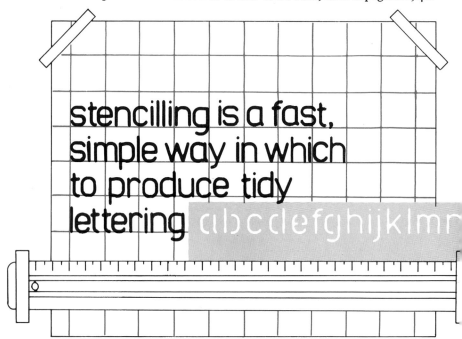

Dry transfer letters

There are three types of dry transfer lettering:
- Ordinary letters for use on paper (not heat resistant).
- Thermal letters for use on paper and film (heat resistant).
- Projection letters for use on film.

Using these letters takes a little time until you get the hang of it, but, properly applied, letters look good. Just adding the title in this lettering can improve the finish of a simple hand-drawn visual.

DRY TRANSFER LETTERS can improve the finished result and are easy to use

Letter style (typeface). The best style for use on visuals is one that is quick and easy to read. Most projection and thermal letters only come in these typefaces, but their letters are available in a vast range of display faces which are unsuitable for projection because

They can be difficult to read quickly

The vowels are too similar

Lightweight serifs do not project well

The recommended styles for projection are Helvetica Medium and Univers, but if you decide to use a more decorative letter, make sure that it can be read at a glance.

Letter size. Dry transfer letters are measured in point sizes (72 points to the inch) or in millimetres.

For projection work, the minimum letter height is 6 mm or 20pt.

72pt   19.3 mm   60pt   16.7 mm   48pt   12.9 mm   36pt 10.1 mm   24pt 6.5 mm   20pt 6 mm

Ordinary dry transfer letters are for use on paper, not film. If applied to film there may be a halo of adhesive surrounding each letter which will show on projection. They are not heat-resistant and cannot be passed unscathed through a thermal copier.

Ordinary Dry Transfer letters can be used for:

- Originals, from which paper copy intermediates are made.
- Diazo master copies.
- Plain paper copier originals.

Thermal dry transfer letters are heat resistant and, if correctly applied, can be used to make several thermal transparencies before the letters deteriorate. If you want to play safe or have to make multi-copies of one transparency, then use an intermediate.

Thermal letters can be used on Diazo masters or may be applied directly to film and projected satisfactorily. But only black letters are available.

APPLYING DRY TRANSFER LETTERS IS REALLY EASY ONCE YOU KNOW HOW — SO JUST FOLLOW THE STEP BY STEP INSTRUCTIONS

Projection transfer letters are available in several projectible colours and are the easiest of the transfer letters to apply directly to film. They are not suitable for thermal copying.

STORE FLAT IN A COOL DRY PLACE

Colours: Black, Red, Green, Yellow, Blue

Storage. All dry transfer letters should be stored flat, with the backing sheet, away from direct sunlight, radiators, or other heat sources.

Applying dry transfer letters
Tools needed – Squared paper, Pencil, Base (Film or paper)
Sheet of letters, Sticky Tape

To keep the letters straight. You will need guidelines on or under the original:
Either
(a)   lightly rule guidelines on to the base in pencil; or
(b)   use a non-reproducible blue or red ruled base for thermal copying; or
(c)   place base over the top of a black ruled grid.
    These guidelines are aligned with either:
a. The dotted lines underneath   b. The base of the letters
    the letters

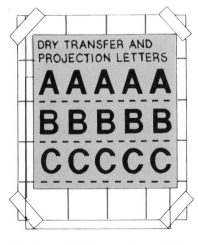
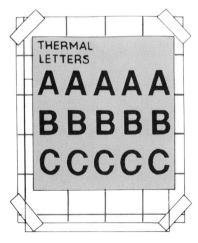

Erasing guidelines. Thermal dry transfer letters are tough and pencil guidelines can be removed with a soft rubber without damaging the letters.

    There is a gap between the dotted guideline and the base of ordinary dry transfer letters which will allow the lines to be erased without touching the letters themselves.

The process

1. Remove the backing sheet and position the first character (letter) on the guideline. Press the character down firmly with an index finger.
2. Using a ballpoint pen, blunt pencil or spatula, gently rub down the character until it lightens or appears to turn grey.
3. Peel back the lettering sheet as you continue to rub gently.

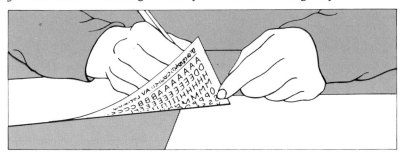

KEEP THE BACKING SHEET UNDERNEATH THE UNUSED PORTION OF LETTERING SHEET TO PREVENT LETTERS FROM BEING TRANSFERRED BY HAND PRESSURE

4. If the character has not transferred completely, lower the sheet and repeat the process.
5. After applying a few letters, lay the backing sheet over the transferred letters and gently burnish to complete adhesion. Use the flat end of a pencil or ballpoint pen to do this.
6. Replace the backing sheet under the lettering sheet and continue.
7. Remove the guidelines with a soft rubber if necessary.

UNWANTED LETTERS CAN BE LIFTED WITH STICKY TAPE

Store sheets of letters flat, with backing sheet, away from direct sunlight or radiators.

Typewriting

Typed transparencies are not the most visually effective nor the most easily visible, but if you use a large type size at least 6 mm (¼ inch) high, and limit the words, you can make a transparency quickly and cheaply. There are direct copy films with a special carbon backing sheet which you can either type on to or draw on to, but no invisible erasing is possible.

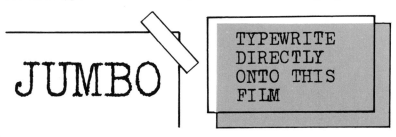

REMEMBER TO USE A CARBON RIBBON FOR THERMAL COPYING.

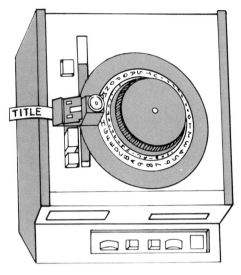

Lettering machines

These machines can be used to print letters and numbers on to strips of self-adhesive film, which can then be placed on to the original and passed through a transparency maker.

The typefaces are larger than those on a typewriter and are faster to produce and apply than are dry transfer letters.

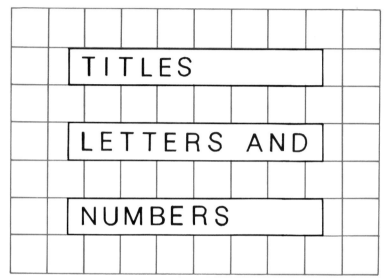

TITLES

LETTERS AND

NUMBERS

Summary
Whichever method you use:

STENCILLING
Dry Transfer Letters
Typewriting

LETTERING MACHINES

It must be NEAT, LEGIBLE IN A STRAIGHT LINE and EASY TO READ QUICKLY FROM THE BACK ROW

4. So what if you can't draw?

For a start, not all visual aids need pictures. Often enough a few words or a simple diagram are all that are needed.

Usually, the visuals are on view for only a short time, and so long as the pictures are easily recognizable and communicate your message, they have done their job.

This section is primarily for those who have difficulty with drawing. However, the clip art section will be useful for anyone who makes their own visuals, whether they can draw or not.

So, whether you choose to draw it yourself or use a little help from other sources, here are some ways to create pictures – even if you can't draw to save your life.

Getting someone else to do it

And if you do not have the time, give this book to your secretary or assistant and let them produce the visuals for you.

SEE PAGE 20 ON HOW TO BRIEF SOMEONE ELSE TO DO THE JOB FOR YOU.

CONTENTS – *Drawing-it-yourself*

- Stick people
- Using shapes

Using a little help

- Reference books; clipping files
- Adjusting size
- Adjusting pictures
- Tracing
- Copying
- Stencils
- Clip art.

Visual comment. Some of the illustrations in this section are explanatory and take the place of a demonstration. In a number of cases they are of necessity detailed, but, in a workshop situation, this section would be practical.

Drawing-it-yourself

Stick people. Stick people are easy to draw and can be made to sit, run, jump, swim, and so forth. In their simplest form, they require a circle for a head, and lines to make a spine, arms, legs and feet. To keep them in proportion, keep the arms, legs and body all to the same length.

The more advanced models bend at the elbows and knees, but they do not need hips nor shoulders, and adding these extras can make them look like stringless marionettes.

Another point to consider is balance. When they run they do, like us, need one leg under or behind the spine to stop them from falling over.

Facial expressions are a matter of a few dots and dashes, while noses can, if necessary, be added to show which way a person is looking.

Using simple shapes. Think of the thing that you want to draw as a collection of geometric shapes: squares, oblongs, triangles, circles, ovals, cones. Then build your picture from a collection of these.

 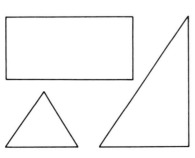 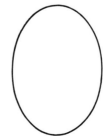 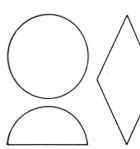

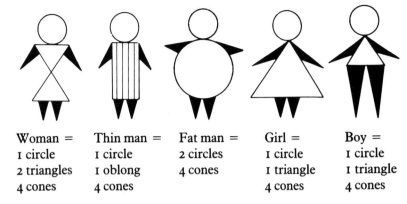

Woman =
1 circle
2 triangles
4 cones

Thin man =
1 circle
1 oblong
4 cones

Fat man =
2 circles
4 cones

Girl =
1 circle
1 triangle
4 cones

Boy =
1 circle
1 triangle
4 cones

Keep your drawing simple and flat (2D), and do not attempt an exact replica of the original. Aim for a simple, recognizable shape. Work out your 'rough' picture on squared paper, and use the rulings as a guideline to help to keep your work in proportion, symmetrical and tidy.

Making them move. Just add a few lines and your object will appear to move. Simple, isn't it?

Using a little help
- Reference books/Clippings files
- Adjusting the size
- Adjusting the picture
- Tracing
- Copying
- Stencils
- Clip art

IF YOU INTEND TAKING A DIRECT COPY FROM ANOTHER PERSON'S WORK, IT IS ADVISABLE TO CHECK COPYRIGHT, TO SEE WHETHER IT APPLIES TO YOUR PARTICULAR APPLICATION

Reference books. Many professional artists refer to books and photographs for visual information – no one can be expected to know what everything looks like and some objects may be difficult to obtain or to keep still long enough for you to sketch them. If you need to do so, never hesitate to work from a photograph or drawing.

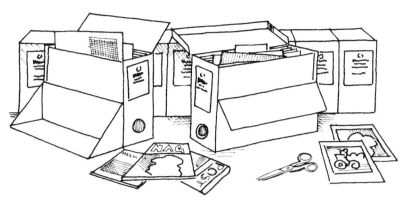

Clippings file. Whenever you see a picture that might come in useful, cut it out and keep it in a clippings file. When you are short of ideas or need a particular illustration, you can then just flip through your file.

Adjusting the size

If your pictures are not the right size or not in proportion to one another, decide on the size you need, and, working within that area, use one of the following methods to enlarge or reduce the originals.

The grid system is a simple way to enlarge or reduce a picture.
1. Rule squares on to the original or paper copy of the original.
2. Lightly rule larger (for enlargement) or smaller (for reduction) squares on to a sheet of paper. Use card for cut-outs and symbols.

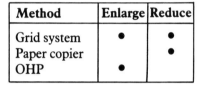

Method	Enlarge	Reduce
Grid system	●	●
Paper copier		●
OHP	●	

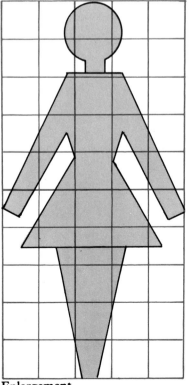

Enlargement

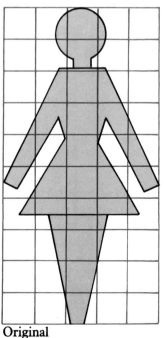

Original

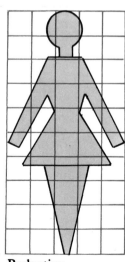

Reduction

3. Use a pencil to copy the original picture square by square.
4. Trace or ink over this copy.
5. Erase pencil marks from inked-in copy.

Paper copier. Some copying machines can be used to make paper copies reduced 50 per cent smaller than the original. If you use this method, check that the reduced copy remains legible enough to be made into a visual.

Paper Copier

Original

Paper Copier

50% Reduction

OHP. This method is useful for flip charts and whiteboards.

1. Make a transparency of the original and project this on to the chart or board.
2. Draw over the projected linework with a suitable pen – to do this you may need to stand slightly to the side of the projected image.
3. If you have difficulty drawing neatly with the board or chart upright, outline the information with a soft pencil, tilt the board or lay the chart flat and ink over your masterpiece in comfort.

Tracing
If the original is the right size, it can be traced.

1. Slip the picture under a sheet of thin paper or film, tape across the corners to prevent the sheets from slipping.
2. Trace, using the correct drawing instrument.

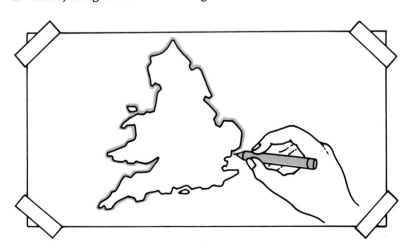

Suitable drawing instruments

Drawing surface	Copying method	Instrument
OHP film	Drawing directly on to film	OHP pen
Clear film	Diazo copier (see pages 53–55)	Opaque black ink Tape
Drafting film	Diazo copier	Opaque black ink Tape
Paper	Thermal copier (see pages 48–52)	Indian ink 2B pencil
Paper	Paper copier (see pages 55–58)	Black ink, OHP pen
Flip chart paper	Drawing directly on to paper	Water-soluble fibre-tip pen

Adjusting the picture

Pictures can be adjusted if they are not quite right; often one character can be used in several ways:

1. Trace the basic outline on to thin paper to get the proportions, position, and so forth.
2. Adjust the outfit – refer to books for details of costumes, uniforms and so on.

  Alternatively, combine tracings from several sources.

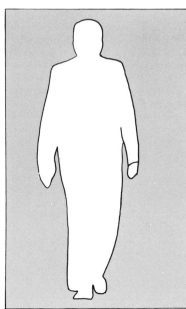

Copying from a printed source

This can be done on one of the transparency makers mentioned on pages 47–58. The copying section comes a bit further on, but let me refer you here to the main points to watch.

1. **Copyright,** see pages 37, 47
2. **Details,** see page 47.

Stencils

There is a variety of plastic stencils and templates available, which provide outlines for maps and chemical apparatus, and also a 'man' stencil with hinged joints. These can all be drawn around with a pen or pencil.

For details of lettering stencils, see page 30.

Clip art

Clip art is an easy way to make visuals that look good. In other words, it is the answer for those who cannot draw. It is done by clipping pictures from various printed sources, or else from books sold specifically for this purpose and to which no copyright applies. The cut-outs are pieced together to make the required picture, then passed through a transparency maker.

A clippings file will be useful here, and can often trigger ideas for ways of presenting the information.

The process

1. Roughly design your visual.
2. Select suitable pictures.
3. Photocopy and cut out, or carefully cut out pictures from a clip-out book, leaving approximately 12 mm (½ inch) around outline.
4. Unless you are working on a non-reproducible grid, place on a suitable base over the 'rough' and stick the cut-outs into position. A dab of glue in one corner is sufficient – avoid wrinkling the papers.
5. Add notes and finish the original.
6. Make intermediates if necessary.
7. Transfer to film.
8. Finish transparency and check on OHP.

IF YOU MAKE A PAPER COPY INTERMEDIATE YOU MAY GET A FAINT SHADOW AROUND THE CUT-OUTS. REFER TO PAGE 57 FOR SOLUTION

Cut out picture

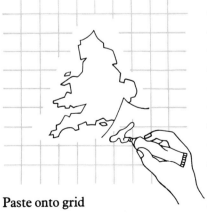

Paste onto grid

Add notes

The techniques described in this chapter might not help you to gain membership of the Royal Academy, but they will help you to produce recognizable drawings for your visual aids.

5. Using colour

Brightly, systematically coloured visuals can help both the audience and the presenter.

Colour can be used to:

1. Aid identification

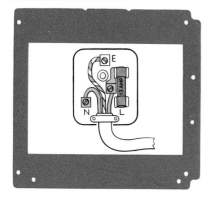

2. Highlight important information

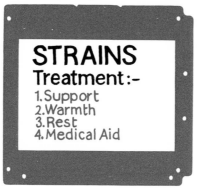

3. Colour code flow paths

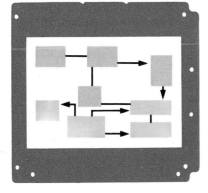

4. Attract attention

5. Reduce eye fatigue

Visual comment: Nos. 1-4 could have been presented on one transparency using the masking system described on page 64. This would have speeded up the presentation and made them easier to compare.

> *FOR MAXIMUM VISUAL IMPACT, THE COLOURS SHOULD BE VIVID AND CONTRASTING*

Pale shades become indistinct when projected in a brightly lit room or over a long viewing distance, and similar tones may be too similar for the viewer to separate the information easily. There are several ways to colour transparencies:

- OHP pens
- Non-adhesive colour film
- Self-adhesive colour film for projection
- Coloured film for use in transparency-making machines
- Colour photography

OHP pens

OHP pens are useful for coloured linework and lettering, but not for large areas of solid colour, since the results are not always satisfactory. If you have no alternative, cross-hatch / / / or use symbols

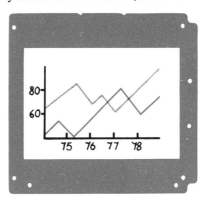

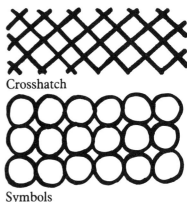

Crosshatch

Symbols

Non-adhesive colour film

Non-adhesive colour film will accept OHP inks and dry transfer lettering and can be used instead of clear film or placed over a black on clear transparency to provide background colour. I suggest that coloured backgrounds should be used for text since the colour, especially yellow, enhances the letters, so making them easier to read.

Shapes can be cut from the colour film to focus the viewers' attention on to the clear sections of the visual.

The colour film is mounted in the frame with the transparency.

FOR ECONOMY, ONE LOOSE SHEET OF SOLID COLOUR CAN BE USED WITH SEVERAL BLACK—LINE-ON-CLEAR VISUALS, JUST PLACE THE COLOUR SHEET OVER THE TRANSPARENCY BEFORE PROJECTING.

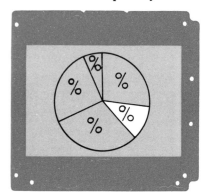

Cutting non-adhesive film

Tools – Sharp blade (scalpel, craft knife)
          Sticky tape
          Cutting card (work on this to avoid damaging desks, etc.)
          Straight edge
Suitable coloured film – Coloured thermal film
                         Various films available from graphics and visual aids suppliers (avoid smoky and very dark colours)

If a paper copy is used as a cutting guide, check that there is no variation in size as a result of the different processes involved.

1. Place a coloured sheet over the transparency or cutting guide and tape across the corners.
2. Carefully cut along the outlines, using the straight edge as a guide if possible.
3. Remove unwanted film.
4. If the coloured film is thick, deeply score the outlines and gently bend the film along the markings to separate.

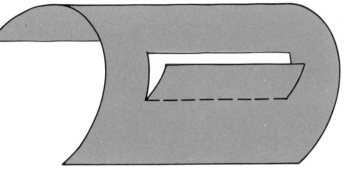

Bend to separate edges

IF YOU ACCIDENTALLY CUT THROUGH THE TRANSPARENCY ITSELF, USE A CLEAR SHEET OF FILM AS A BACKING SHEET AND FRAME THE TRANSPARENCY BETWEEN THE COLOUR AND CLEAR FILM

Self-adhesive colour

There are several suitable films available which have the special adhesive needed for projection work. (The wrong adhesives project, so giving the colour a cloudy or murky effect.)

Self-adhesive projection film comes in a range of basic, bright colours and should be stored flat in a cool, dry place. It can be used on large or small areas and is easy to apply once you know how to do it.

Tools – Scissors
       Sharp blade
       Sticky tape
       Straight edge
       Cutting card

TO PREVENT DAMAGE TO TABLES AND DESKS, WORK ON A CUTTING BOARD

1. Tape the transparency to the cutting card to keep it flat.
2. Use scissors to cut a piece of film slightly larger than the area which is to be coloured.
3. Remove the backing sheet from the film.
4. Place the film over the area to be coloured. If wrinkles or air bubbles occur, peel back the film and reapply, or lightly smooth out bubbles with a soft cloth when burnishing (step 7).
5. Cut round the outline, using the straight edge as a guide where possible.
6. Remove and discard excess film.
7. Lightly rub over the colour with a soft cloth or tissue.
8. If you accidentally cut through the transparency, place a sheet of clear film underneath it then frame.

Colouring by transparency maker

There are various films available for these machines:

Black line on colour

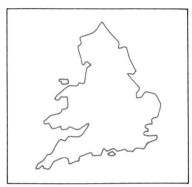

Colour line on clear

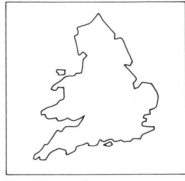

Black line on clear

Reverse image

And full details of original requirements are given in the reprographics section (see pages 49, 54, 56).

Colour photography

This requires full-colour artwork or subject. It can be expensive to use, but is impressive under the right circumstances, as when dealing with product presentations and other promotional work. However, the basic rules still apply.

6. Reprographics

There are several ways to transfer originals on to film, and these are the DIY transparency-making processes:

- THERMAL copying
- DIAZO copying
- PLAIN PAPER (electrostatic/xerographic) copying

All three methods are simple, but you should refer to the operating instructions for your particular machine as these vary slightly from make to make.

THE QUALITY OF THE COPY DEPENDS ON THE QUALITY OF THE ORIGINAL (MASTER) IRRESPECTIVE OF THE PROCESS USED

There are two points to watch when copying printed materials:

1. **Copyright** – the laws are complex, so I must leave it to you to decide whether copyright applies in your situation.
2. **Suitability of original** – book illustrations and handouts may contain many details and still be effective because the readers can pace their reading speed to suit themselves. The length of time that a visual is on view is limited, so the content needs to be kept to the essential points.

If a printed original is complex, remove unnecessary details and check the text and captions for readability before transferring to film.

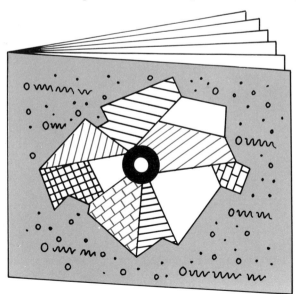

OK for a book

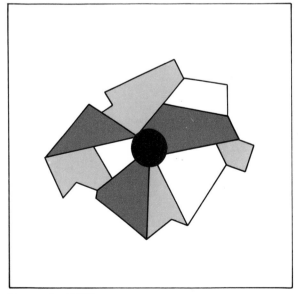

Better for OHP

Thermal copying

Functions of a thermal copier. The thermal copier has several different but complementary functions. Apart from lamination, the original requirements are identical, so that matching handouts and transparencies can be produced.

Since this book is primarily concerned with visuals, I shall concentrate on the transparency-making process.

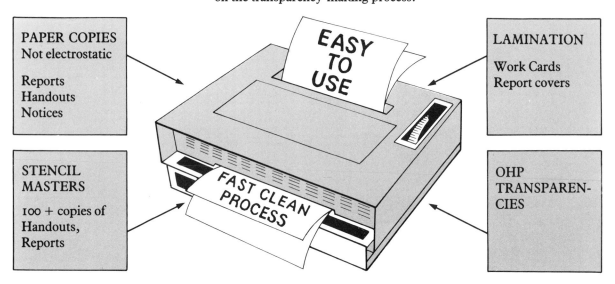

PAPER COPIES
Not electrostatic

Reports
Handouts
Notices

STENCIL MASTERS

100 + copies of Handouts, Reports

LAMINATION

Work Cards
Report covers

OHP TRANSPAREN-CIES

EASY TO USE

FAST CLEAN PROCESS

The process. Thermal copying is fast, clean (no chemicals) and relies on heat from an infra-red lamp which is directed on to the original document, to be reflected in turn by the darker (carbon-containing) areas on to a heat-sensitive film or paper.

The films are not light-sensitive; consequently the copier can be used in normal light conditions.

HEAT SOURCE

IMAGE

Heat sensitive film

Paper original

In brief, the process involves placing a sheet of specially coated film over the original and passing both through the copier. With some thermal copiers, it is necessary to use a carrier to protect the original and the film.

Maintenance. Little maintenance is required, but occasionally the glass roller or plastic conveyor belt should be cleaned since specks of dust and other marks on the belt or roller may reproduce on the copies. Other repairs should be left to a technician.

Original for thermal copying. Not all materials reproduce thermographically, so I have compiled a checklist for you.

Original checklist

Requirements	Recommendations
Writing materials Areas for reproduction need carbon mineral content	*Use* graphite pencil (2B) Inks – black, drawing, indian or duplicating. Carbon typewriter ribbon. Black printing. Black dry transfer letters.
Base Tints may cause background shadows M/C does not accept books	*Use* matt white paper *Make* and use intermediate copy
Solid areas of colour May reproduce poorly	*Either* trace original outline only *or* use paper copy of original, draw around colour areas, cut out inside of area, back up copy with sheet of white paper and cross-hatch area or add solid colour to transparency.
Mixed originals Containing ball point and coloured inks (e.g. letters) may not reproduce in full	*Use* intermediate, see page 51.
Size No enlargement/reduction possible	*Use* same size original *or* use photographic intermediate and adjust size at this stage

Altering originals. Use intermediate copies of valuable originals.
1. Cut out unwanted areas carefully.
2. Place sheet of white paper behind original or intermediate.
3. Make any additions.
4. Re-film, keeping backing sheet in place.

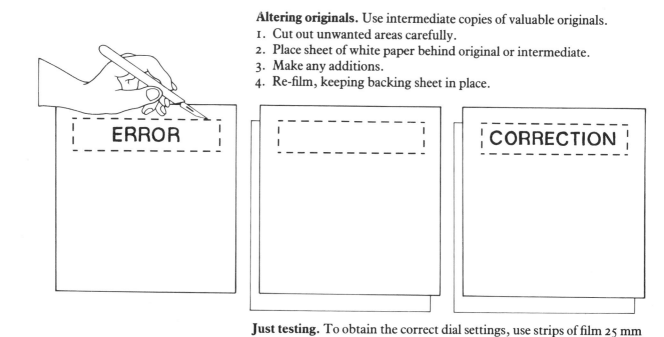

Just testing. To obtain the correct dial settings, use strips of film 25 mm (1 inch) wide, rather than waste a complete sheet of film.

Thermal troubleshooter 1

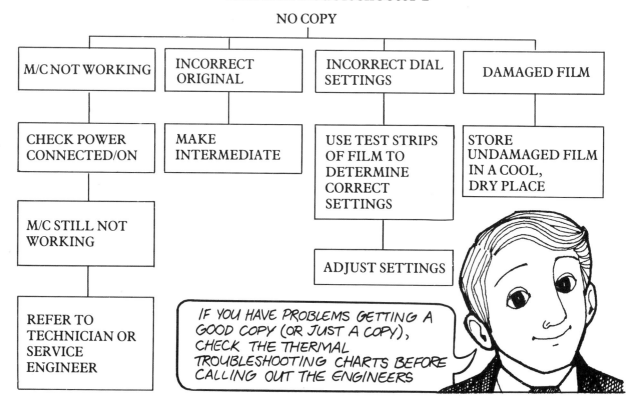

NO COPY

| M/C NOT WORKING | INCORRECT ORIGINAL | INCORRECT DIAL SETTINGS | DAMAGED FILM |

CHECK POWER CONNECTED/ON

MAKE INTERMEDIATE

USE TEST STRIPS OF FILM TO DETERMINE CORRECT SETTINGS

STORE UNDAMAGED FILM IN A COOL, DRY PLACE

M/C STILL NOT WORKING

ADJUST SETTINGS

REFER TO TECHNICIAN OR SERVICE ENGINEER

IF YOU HAVE PROBLEMS GETTING A GOOD COPY (OR JUST A COPY), CHECK THE THERMAL TROUBLESHOOTING CHARTS BEFORE CALLING OUT THE ENGINEERS

Thermal troubleshooter 2 (POOR OR UNSATISFACTORY COPIES)

Problem	Cause	Solution
Faint letters/lines	Incorrect setting (under-exposed) Insufficient carbon content	Adjust settings (slower=darker) Use intermediate
Heavy fuzzy lines/ letters closed in	Incorrect setting (over-exposed)	Adjust setting (faster=lighter)
Background shadows	Tinted background on original Dirty roller/conveyor belt	Adjust for over exposure to lighten shadows Clean roller/belt
Incomplete reproduction	Large areas of solid colour on original Insufficient carbon content Mixed original	Alter original (see page 49) Use intermediate (see page 49) Use intermediate (see page 49)

Intermediates are used if the original is unsuitable, fragile or valuable. For thermal copying use, either:
- Photographic (black/white) copies, or
- Electrostatic paper copies of the original.

'Rough' guidelines. There are various printed grids, ruled in blue or red, which make a suitable, non-reproducible base for a 'rough'. Some inks contain more black than others, which is why I recommend you to test the grid first and then to stick to whichever brand proves most useable; test the pencils you use in a similar way.

THERMAL COPIERS DO NOT REPRODUCE ALL COLOURS—AN ADVANTAGE WHEN PREPARING ROUGHS

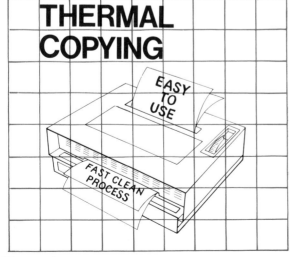

The rough

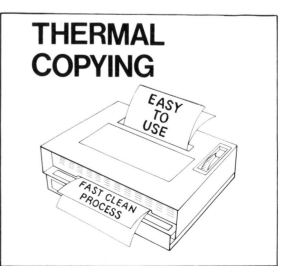

The transparency

Moreover, clip art and thermal letters can be used on the rough. The rough markings need not be erased for thermal transparency making, but may reproduce on an intermediate paper copy. Again, this is a matter of trial and error, since not all paper copiers see blue either. If non-reproducible materials are unavailable, use a black pencil and grid for the rough and trace on to thin paper.

THE 'ROUGH' CAN BE DRAWN IN A NON-REPRODUCIBLE COLOUR ON A NON-REPRODUCIBLE BASE, AND INKED OVER WITH ONE OF THE MATERIALS MENTIONED ON PAGE 22.

Films for thermal copying

Black line on clear.

Colour line on clear.

Black line on colour.

Reverse image.

Dual purpose film masters (use with carbons to transfer several colours to one sheet).

Projection units (allow more than one colour to be put on to one sheet of film).

Also available – Paper for copying
  Masters for spirit duplicating/lamination film.

Diazo copying

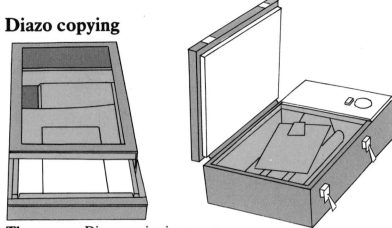

The process. Diazo copying is a two-stage process:
1. **Printing** – the master and Diazo film are exposed to controlled ultra-violet light which passes through the clear areas on the original to bleach out the dye on the film underneath.
   Although the Diazo film is light-sensitive, it can be exposed for short handling periods without suffering damage.

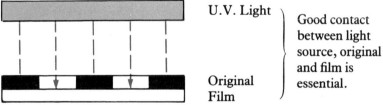

U.V. Light

Original Film

Good contact between light source, original and film is essential.

2. **Developing** – the film copy is suspended over dyeline strength ammonia vapour.

Maintenance
1. **Printer** – clean the glass platen with methylated spirit.
2. **Developer** (called processor by some manufacturers) – keep the ammonia up to strength with regular topping up and cleaning out of dead liquor.

Film storage. Store in a cool, dark place, preferably under refrigeration. This will increase its shelf life.

Density settings. Processing speeds vary according to the make and colour of film and type of machinery used. To determine density settings, do a series of tests using strips of film and make a reference chart.

Originals. Originals must be transparent or translucent. (Translucent originals take longer to expose.)
   There are two ways to obtain suitable originals:
1. Photographically
2. By working directly on to film.

Diazo original checklist

Requirements	Recommendations
Photographic Make positive film copies from camera-ready artwork	Photograph and make high-contrast litho film master copy from linework, dry transfer letters, solid colour areas and shading patterns *Avoid* half-tones
Direct drawing base	*Use* clear film or drafting film
Writing materials Must have high actinic blocking content	*Use* pressure-sensitive tapes rather than ink; if none available, use dense black drawing ink. Dry transfer letters and shading patterns
Solid areas of colour	*Use* photo opaquing films and fluids or cut-out, blackout masks from black card/paper and stick it in place with spray adhesive or double-sided tape.
Shaded areas	*Use* pressure-sensitive shading patterns

PENCIL GUIDELINES, ETC, MUST BE ERASED BEFORE FILMING

To update an original make alterations on artwork and rephotograph or amend direct film copy.

Diazo troubleshooters. Good copies are a matter of good originals and good housekeeping. If the machines are in order, the ammonia fluids clean and up to strength, then there are only a few checks which need to be made.

1. The original ⟶	Refer checklist for details ⟶	Make photographic intermediate of unsuitable original or re-draw
2. Exposure settings ⟶	Faster = darker Slower = lighter ⟶	Do test using strips of film
3. Poor copy ⟶	Film emulsion side to face master copy ⟶	Re-film

Rough guidelines. The easiest way to keep lettering straight is to place the film base over a black-ruled grid and then there will be no guidelines to erase.

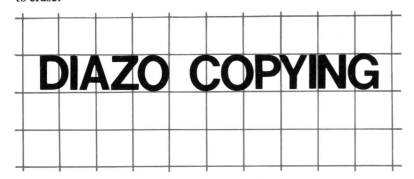

Some Diazo film available
Black line on clear, yellow, pink, blue, green background
Red line on clear, violet, green, brown, orange, yellow, cyan, double black

Plain paper (xerographic) copying

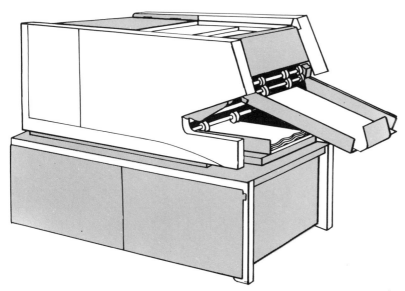

The process. Plain paper (xerographic) copiers have a drum or master in the machine which retains an electrostatic charge. The copy is first made on the drum and then transferred to uncoated paper or film. These paper copies cannot be used as intermediates for thermal copying.

This type of copier should not be confused with direct electrostatic copiers which need a zinc-oxide-coated paper to retain the electrostatic charge. Since film will not hold zinc oxide, it is impossible to make transparencies by this method. However, paper copies from these machines can be used as intermediates for thermal copying.

Maintenance. Clean the glass platen with duplicator or methylated spirit to remove marks.

All other repairs should be left to a service engineer.

Originals. Transparencies can be made from virtually any original, including books, photographs, 3D objects.

Better results are obtained from black on white master copies, but if colour is used, avoid pastel tones.

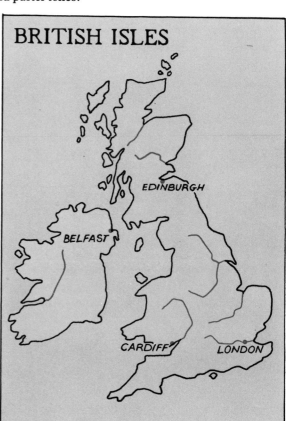

The left hand illustration gives the best results

Original checklist

Suitable originals	Recommendations
Black lines/lettering on white gives best results	*Avoid* large areas of solid black; see thermal copying checklist, page 49, for solution
Coloured originals Reproduce as black or grey	*Avoid* pastel tones

Problem originals. PPCs reproduce the shadows around the edge of paste-up artwork (clip art is paste-up). The solution is to make a paper copy, remove the shadows with correcting fluid, re-copy and use this copy as the master for transparency making.

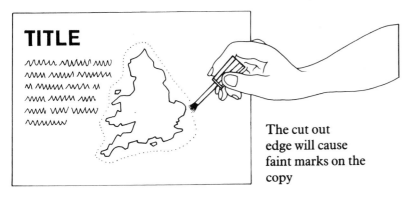

The cut out edge will cause faint marks on the copy

Add colour with self-adhesive film or OHP pens – the latter can prove difficult to remove from the now chemically coated film.

PPC trouble-shooters. Plain paper copiers are simple to operate, but I have compiled a checklist in case you have any difficulty obtaining a good film copy (transparency).

Problem	Solution
Copy too light Copy too dark	Adjust density controls
Oily residue on transparency	Wipe off with tissue
Image not fused to film	Machine needs service
Wrinkled transparency	(a) Allow machine to cool down (b) Leave transparency in tray until cool before handling (c) Use thicker film (d) If this fails, call service engineer
Background shadows	(a) Clean glass platen with spirit (b) Adjust density control
Copies sticking together	(a) Feed film sheets into M/C individually (b) Interleave with paper (use paper copies to refer to during presentation) (c) If this fails, call service engineer

Roughs for PPCs. Although some PPCs do not see blue, some do, so test your copier to determine whether or not you can use the blue grid system mentioned on page 51. If you cannot, then use a black-ruled grid for the 'rough' and trace on to thin paper. Erase any unwanted pencil marks from the master copy with a soft rubber.

Films available
Black line on clear, as in illustration on page 52.
Black line on colour.

Other processes

To complete the reprographics picture, here are the processes that can be bought in from outside agencies.

- **Screen or litho printing** is done by a few specialist printers and is suitable for runs of 50 to 100 or more copies off each original.
- **Colour copying** from colour originals is undertaken by a few copying bureaux. The colour reproduction is not always accurate and the machine manufacturers recommend using primary or complementary colours for best results.
- **Colour photography** can be an expensive process, but, provided the original is good, the results will be good too.

For full details of original requirements for the above three processes, consult with the printer, copy bureau or photographer beforehand.

Summary

Check copyright and
Original suitability when copying from
Printed materials.
Intermediates preserve fragile originals.
Easy DIY
Reprographics systems . . .

THERMAL, DIAZO
AND PLAIN PAPER
COPYING

7. Transparencies

Framing transparencies

Framing transparencies makes them easier to handle and to store. Once they are mounted in card frames, they can be filed in special presentation binders. (See page 60 for other systems.)

Some frames have a press-out centre ruled with squares to help with alignment. Alternatively:

1. Place frame face down over squared paper and align the inside of the frame with the squares. (Your rough can be used as a framing guide).

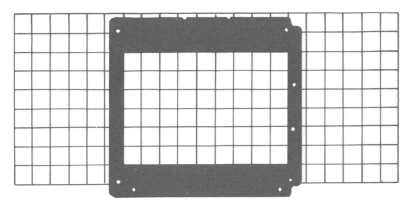

See page 63 for framing overlays.

2. Position visual face down over the frame, using the squares to align the frame and the visual.
3. Tape visual neatly across corners to attach it to the frame (sticky tape projects).
4. Turn the transparency the right way round and add masks or alignment marks for reveals.
5. Add title, transparency number and brief lecture notes in writing that is large and legible enough for the presenter to be able to read it while the transparency is in use.

In general, it is better to place the film on the back of the frame so as to avoid distortion, but accurate alignment of overlays is easier if it is placed on the front; see page 63.

Updating transparencies

Visuals need to be amended or brought up to date as and when new information becomes available.

Additions can sometimes be made directly on to the transparency itself, and so long as the alterations are consistent with the style of the original information, the updatings will not be obvious.

See page 50 for amending originals.

Storing transparencies

Keep transparencies in a cool, dry place since moisture can cause the film to wrinkle.

I use the frame boxes for filing transparencies, putting the original artwork in an envelope at the back.

LP record cases may also be used, and these make useful carrying cases for presentations.

Transparency binders. There are a variety of systems on the market, and some binders contain plastic wallets for both visuals and notes. The visual is projected in the wallet, and this provides extra protection from handling and for storing. The overlay system is not, however, easy to use with this method of presentation.

The transparency folds back into the binder after use.

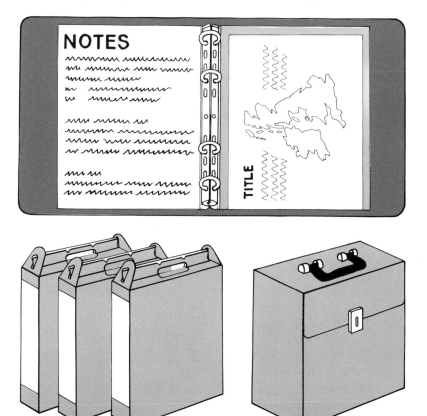

8. Display techniques

Visually complex information can be difficult for the presenter to convey and for the audience to comprehend easily. The end result can all too easily be confusion and/or boredom.

To overcome this problem, there are display techniques which can be used to show complicated subjects in easy stages and which allow the presenter to pace the rate at which the information is put on view according to the needs of individual groups of people.

THESE TECHNIQUES CAN HELP TO MAKE THE PRESENTATION VISUALLY MORE INTERESTING, AND TO GAIN AND HOLD THE ATTENTION OF THE AUDIENCE – A BENEFIT NOT TO BE OVERLOOKED

Visual aid	Display technique
OHP	Overlay Mask Reveal Animation
Flip Chart	Building up information See pages 74, 89
Whiteboards	Build-ups See pages 80, 89

Overhead projector display techniques
- OVERLAY
- MASK
- REVEAL
- ANIMATION

Overlay technique

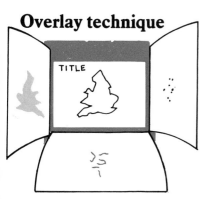

The overlay technique is used for a step-by-step breakdown or build-up of information. The transparency has a base picture which shows such elementary facts as outlines, a title, or the first stage in a process. The overlaying sheets of film contain the additional data, separated into its component parts. These are taped to the frame and can be overlaid in any sequence to build up the complete picture.

Producing overlays. The accurate alignment of overlays is important, and a punch bar will be useful for keeping the individual sheets in place while you work. Satisfactory overlays can, however, be produced without any special equipment.

Production procedure. Working within the frame area. (See page 23):
1. Prepare a 'rough' of the transparency, including notes, and mark the position and size of clip-art cut-outs.
2. Put a small + in corners just outside the frame area.

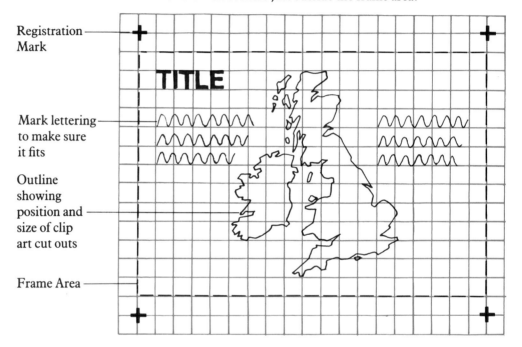

Registration Mark

Mark lettering to make sure it fits

Outline showing position and size of clip art cut outs

Frame Area

3. Using different colours for each overlay sheet, mark the information separation.
   This system is particularly useful when the separate information is scattered about the sheet or if the final production is to be undertaken by someone else.

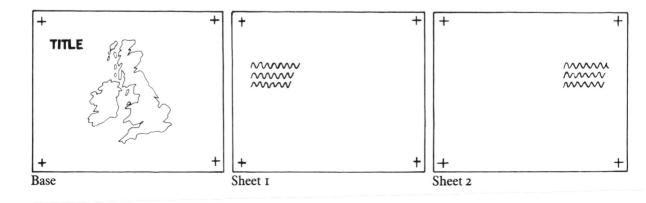

Base   Sheet 1   Sheet 2

4. Transfer each section (including +) to separate, suitable bases for reproduction or, alternatively, trace directly on to AV film.

Reproduction method	Suitable base
Thermal copying copying	Paper
Diazo copying	Film Paper
Plain paper copying	Paper

If the breakdown needs to be apparent when the picture is complete, use different line colours for each overlay sheet.

5. Mount the base sheet on top of frame and tape across the corners.
6. Add overlaying sheets using + for alignment. Tape film into position along the opposite edges. If necessary, trim so that they lie flat when closed.

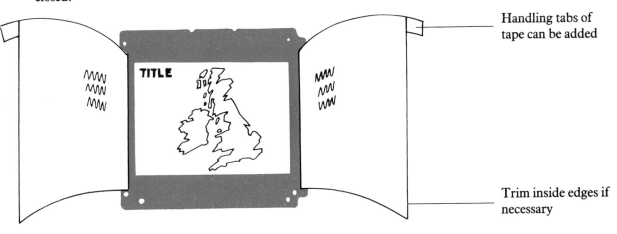

Handling tabs of tape can be added

Trim inside edges if necessary

Between four to six sheets of film can be overlayed on most OHPs, but if you intend using a flat projector where the light source is in the head, check first to see how many sheets can be overlayed before the projected image dims.

HOWEVER, TWO OR MORE OVERLAYS ARE SUFFICIENT FOR MOST PURPOSES. MORE THAN THAT CAN BE DIFFICULT TO ALIGN AND HANDLE

Masking

These windows
can be overlapped to
prevent gaps – but
will then have to be
opened in sequence

The masking technique allows individual blocks of information to be shown independently from one another – yet another way to show the steps in a process, unfold a story or prevent the audience from reading ahead of you. The masks are made from card or from paper hinged to the frame with tape, and can usually be opened in any sequence; it is helpful to have a note on each 'window' of what lies underneath, just in case you forget or someone else has to use the transparency.

Production procedure. Working within the frame area:
1. Plan 'rough' transparency, including notes and so forth.
2. Mark masking division on the rough.
3. Transfer information (less the dividing lines) to film.
4. Frame the transparency, using the rough as a guide.
5. To make masks, cut carefully along the dividing lines on the rough.
6. Tape the masks into position.

This technique has most visual impact for text if the base is black. To obtain this, use a reverse-image film or paper blackout mask; see page 24.

The masks need not
be so accurate –
there will be no
white gaps

Reveals

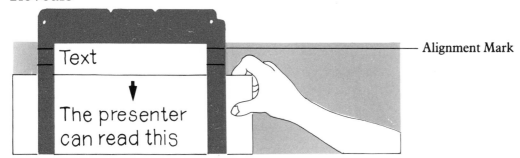

— Alignment Mark

Revealing is a simple but effective way of focusing the audience's attention on to what you want them to see and when you want them to see it. Displaying one line or section of text at a time stops the viewers from reading ahead and possibly not giving their full attention to what is being said as at that particular moment.

It is, however, better to show a section of several lines that make sense than one that does not, and the alignment marks on the frame will act as a reminder of where each division ends.

Simply place a sheet of paper underneath the transparency and pull it towards yourself, aligning the paper with marks on the frame to keep it straight.

Production procedure. Working within frame area on squared paper:
1. Roughly lay out text (space lines allowing room for paper reveal). This will save production time since it is difficult to estimate the exact amount of space needed.
2. Produce transparency and frame.
3. Put alignment marks on frame, underneath last line of each section.

> I've spent ages producing this transparency and I've run out of spa

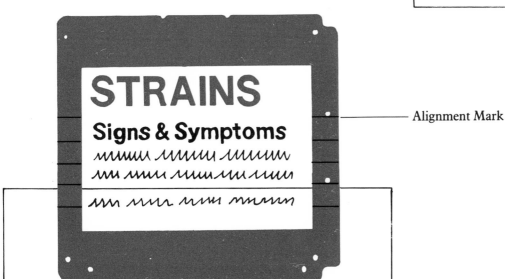

— Alignment Mark

Colour can be used to separate blocks of text visually.

SOME OF THE TECHNIQUES IN THIS SECTION TAKE TIME TO PREPARE, BUT IN THE RIGHT SITUATION THE RESULT IS BOTH VISUALLY AND COST EFFECTIVE

Animation – on the move with OHP

Although the OHP is usually associated with static pictures, basic and simulated motion are possible. Besides the advantage of seeing things in action, moving pictures can help to attract and hold the attention of an audience.

The applications are varied, but to give you some ideas I have listed a few of those topics which I have used or seen 'on the move'.

- Mechanical movement (2- and 4-stroke engine cycles)
- Science experiments (magnetic force fields)
- Mathematics (slide rules)
- Flow paths (cash flows, road safety, various processes)
- First aid, biology (circulation)
- Business and other games (chess, brain teasers such as moving coins and matchsticks)
- Puppetry (useful for story telling and language teaching)

OHP animation falls into two categories:

1. **Manual** – objects and models are manipulated by the presenter.
2. **Simulated** – an optical illusion of movement is created by moving one specially marked film over another at a fixed speed.

Manual animation

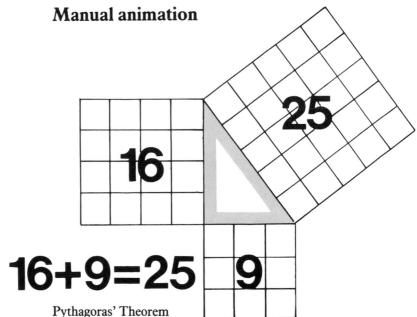

Pythagoras' Theorem

Moving shapes and letters. Shapes, letters and numbers may be cut from coloured film (or card for a silhouette effect) and used for spelling games or simple arithmetic. They can be moved by hand or pushed into position with a pointer.

For a one-off application, the base outline can be drawn on to the film roll, but if the visual is to be used often, draw the base on to a sheet of film and keep the shapes in an envelope pinned to the frame.

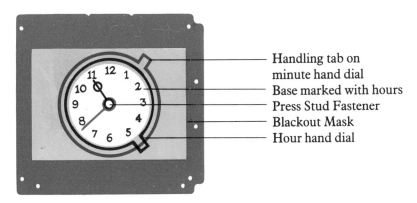

Handling tab on
minute hand dial
Base marked with hours
Press Stud Fastener
Blackout Mask
Hour hand dial

Clockwork. A transparency clock can be made from three sheets of film marked with the relevant information and joined in the centre with a press stud (when you punch the central hole, allow play for easy movement). This technique can be extended to circular calculators, dials, cogs and wheels.

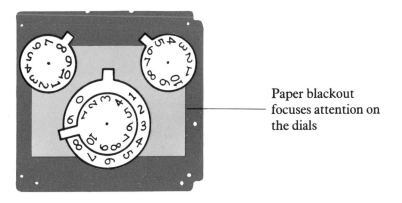

Paper blackout
focuses attention on
the dials

The clocks should not overlap one another, but can overlap into the frame area.

And, for language teaching, discs displaying words and pictures may be used.

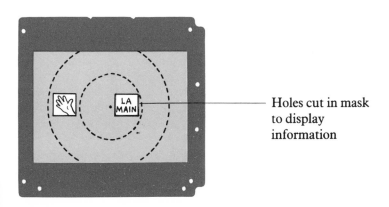

Holes cut in mask
to display
information

To align the words and pictures, fix the sheets of film together with a press stud, rotate each disc to the correct window position and add information.

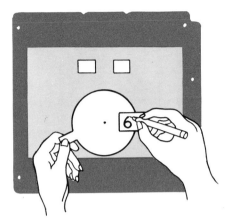

Overlay. Several overlaying sheets can be used to simulate movement when flipped quickly on to the screen. I have seen this used to great effect to show the various body positions of an athlete in action. The picture can also be built up slowly and the individual movements discussed one by one.

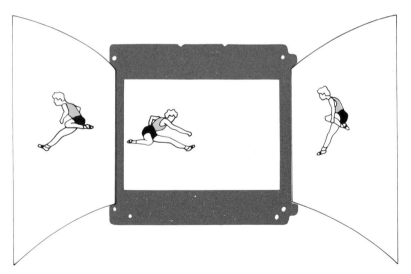

Moving-parts models. These are more complicated to produce than the previous transparencies, but are well worth the effort when they are needed to convey technical information.

Models can be made from Perspex, but this is difficult to cut. I have made satisfactory mobile models from film, matchsticks, card, drawing pins and string.

However, ready-made kits and models are available which cover such subjects as trigonometry, 2- and 4-stroke engine cycles, pressure gauges, slide and log rules.

DIY moving models. Thermometers and **sliding scales** can be made using a base film marked with the relevant details and a moving strip of film which is kept in position by matchstick runners stuck to the frame; the strip (representing the mercury) will need several inches of blank film at either end for easy handling.

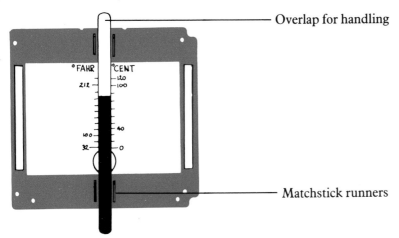

Overlap for handling

Matchstick runners

Archimedes principle could be demonstrated by sliding a sheet of coloured film between runners; the outline could be of a water tank or bath, and the moving mass could be a matchbox or the silhouette of a man.

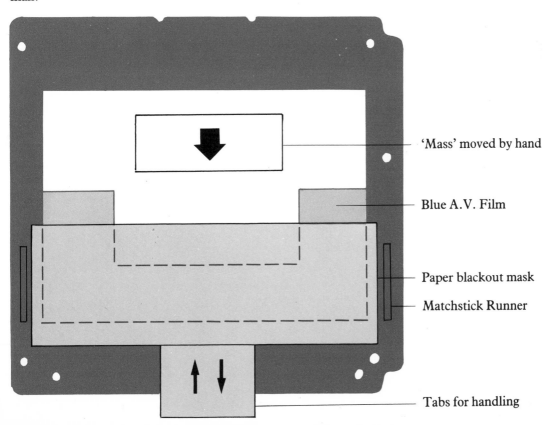

'Mass' moved by hand

Blue A.V. Film

Paper blackout mask

Matchstick Runner

Tabs for handling

Simulated movement. This can be quite spectacular. The optical illusion of movement is created by applying a self-adhesive film, printed with the appropriate movement (flows, turbulence, spinning and so on) to the transparency, and then:

1. Spinning a polarising disc between the transparency and projector head.
2. Winding a printed film roll underneath the transparency.

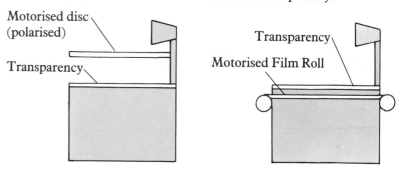

The equipment is not interchangeable, and for further information I suggest that you contact your local visual aids supplier or the manufacturers.

Summary
Types of movement
- Moving shapes and letters
- Clockwork and dials
- Overlays
- Moving parts models
- Simulated movement

9. The non-projected visual aids

- FLIP CHARTS
- WHITEBOARDS – Wet wipe
  Dry wipe
  Magnetic

The non-projected aids are another effective DIY communication tool and can be used on their own or in conjunction with a projected aid; see page 89. They are best suited for use in small or average-size rooms since the information on boards and charts may not be easily seen from the back row of a lecture theatre.

The information that is common to both media follows; individual points are listed under each aid.

Software chart for whiteboards and flip charts

Product	How to use	Details	Available from AV supplier	Artshop	Comments
Flip chart pads	page 72		●		Different pad for each type of easel
Newsprint paper	page 72	Sold loose in sheets		●	Cheap – clip to board with bulldog clips or drawing-board clips
Suitable markers	pages 73, 76	Wide range of colours for charts	●	●	Use broad-tipped brightly coloured markers. Water soluble best for charts
		Special pens for boards	●		Water-soluble spirit-based and dry wipe available
Cleaning fluids	page 75	Liquid or spray	●		For use with spirit-based inks. (Do not use household or abrasive cleaners)
Magnetic accessories	pages 77, 78, 79	Tiles, tapes, symbols, discs, letters, self-adhesive tapes	●		
Dry-transfer letters	pages 30, 76		●	●	Use large, easy-to-read typeface
Coloured card and paper	page 79			●	Use vibrant, contrasting colours

Drawing and lettering guide

For a viewing distance of 9 metres (30 feet):

LETTER HEIGHT – 50 mm (2 inch) capitals
38 mm (1½ inches) lower case 'x' height

LINESPACING – 62 mm (2½ inches) between bottom of one line and top of next.

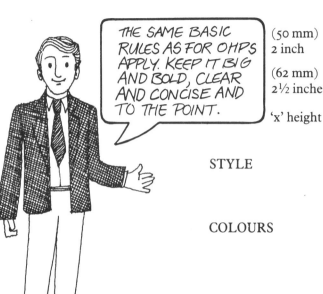

(50 mm) 2 inch

(62 mm) 2½ inches

'x' height

CAPITALS

lower case

STYLE – *BOLD,* legible and in a straight line.
PRINT if your handwriting is not up to scratch (after a while your charts will be easier to read than your memos to colleagues).

COLOURS – *VIBRANT AND CONTRASTING* – the more delicate hues will not be visible from the back.
Forget realism, make sure that the audience can see the information.

DRAWING STYLE – *THE SIMPLER THE BETTER.* See page 26 for OHP graphics section. Also page 38 for adjusting the size.

Presenting the information

1. Move along long boards while you write. Hold the pen with the tip pointing downwards to obtain continuous flow of ink.
2. Keep the layout structured. Try not to cram every available space with information or write at an angle.
3. Talk to the audience, not the aid.
4. Stand aside and point. Use a thin pointer rather than your arm, which could obscure some of the notes.

Flip charts (newsprint)

Custom-made flip charts are similar to large writing pads which have two holes along the top edge to hook them on to the easel.

Newsprint is a cheap paper available in large sheets which can be clipped to a stiff backing (an old blackboard or piece of hardboard) with bulldog or drawing-board clips.

The pages can be prepared in advance or used during the presentation for *ad hoc* notes and diagrams. When the page in use is no longer needed, it should be flipped back over the support or it will create a distraction for the audience.

Alternatively, the pages can be used as wallcharts.

Easels: the ready-made charts have their own lightweight easels, but a wooden blackboard easel will do for newsprint and the back of a chair can be used as a support if nothing else is available.

Setting up flip charts

1. Adjust the height to allow the presenter to work in comfort and the audience to see clearly.
2. Remember to leave a blank page at the front and several blanks in between the prepared charts in case you need to make impromptu notes.

Guidelines can be drawn in faintly in pencil and will only be on view to the presenter.

Reading between the lines: faint, memory-jogging notes can be written between the lines of lettering on prepared charts and are easier to read than cue cards or a script.

THE PROCESS
Step 1
Insert legible
Step 2
notes here

Inks for flip charts

The water-soluble, broad-tipped markers are best since spirit-based inks can seep through the page and spoil the sheet underneath. OHP markers are suitable, as are any of the vast range of fibre-tips sold by stationers and art shops.

AVOID PALE SHADES

Display techniques

Flip charts are not so versatile as the OHP or whiteboard, but a simple build-up technique is possible.

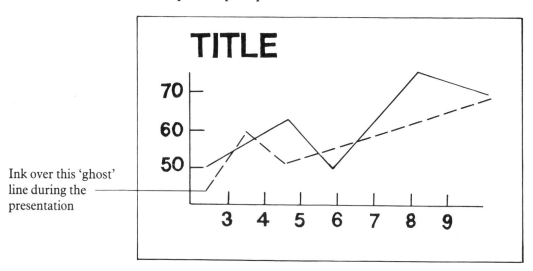

Ink over this 'ghost' line during the presentation

To emphasize points, extra information can be added to flip charts during the presentation. Work in pencil and lightly draw in the additions beforehand, then ink over these markings during the talk. This technique is useful for graphs; see page 89.

Storage. Flip charts can be rolled or folded and are readily portable.

It is possible to use the same chart several times before it becomes too dishevelled, but do not expect charts to last as long as transparencies.

Summary

Flip unwanted sheets over back of support.
Leave blanks for
Impromptu notes between
Prepared sheets.

Colours – vibrant and contrasting
Height of letters – 2 inch (50 mm) minimum
Adjust height of easel to suit presenter.
Read between lines
To save using/losing
Script or cue cards.

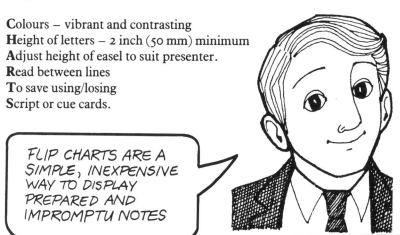

Whiteboards

There are two types of whiteboard surface:

- WET WIPE
- DRY WIPE

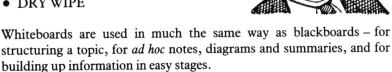

EITHER SURFACE CAN BE MOUNTED ONTO A METAL CORE TO MAKE A MAGNET BOARD

Whiteboards are used in much the same way as blackboards – for structuring a topic, for *ad hoc* notes, diagrams and summaries, and for building up information in easy stages.

   Whiteboards are easier to clean than blackboards and they provide a better background for colour.

Cleaning is only a matter of using the correct cleaning fluids or erasers so that the surface materials will not become damaged.

Board cleaners

Surface	Writing material	Cleaner
Wet wipe	Water-soluble ink Spirit-based ink	Damp cloth or tissue Special cleaner (spray or liquid)
Dry wipe	Dry-wipe ink Spirit-based ink	Soft cloth or tissue Special cleaner

AVOID ABRASIVE CLEANERS

Types of board. Whiteboards can be wall-mounted or free-standing units containing one or more of the surfaces. The mobile, free-standing units rotate through 360 degrees, so allowing the presenter to use both sides of the board or to tilt it to make a screen for the OHP (I find it easier to work on a tilted board when I am preparing diagrams.) There are rolls of self-adhesive fabric which may be applied to a rigid backing, such as hardboard or metal sheeting, to make an inexpensive whiteboard; or you could use this material to resurface a damaged board.

Writing on the board. To obtain a continuous flow of ink, hold the pen with the tip facing downwards. No pressure is needed, but remember to replace the cap immediately after use to avoid the tip from drying out.

Guidelines can be ruled faintly in pencil on to the board.

Dry transfer letters can be applied to boards. This can be time-consuming for a one-off application, but will give a professional look to more 'permanent' aids.

Wet-wipe boards. The board surface is designed for use with water-soluble markers. The inks can be erased with a damp cloth, though the board surface should then be left to dry before re-use or the new markings may run.

Spirit markers can be used for more permanent work, but will need a special solvent to remove them from the board without damaging the surface.

Charting and permanent displays of information. Permanent outlines and base information can be drawn with a spirit-based marker, the variable information being added in water-soluble ink. The non-permanent ink can then be removed without damage to the standard chart or outline.

WORK PLAN					
DAY	A	B	C	D	E
⟿					
⟿					
⟿					
⟿					

Another use for this technique is critical-path analysis.

Dry-wipe boards need dry-wipe markers, which contain a special ink. This is erased with a dry cloth or tissue, leaving the surface immediately ready for re-use. If the board has been cleaned incorrectly or the surface damaged, the dry-wipe inks may 'ghost' or leave shadow markings. Therefore if your board is in pristine condition, try to keep it that way.

If it becomes badly damaged, you could resurface it, using the self-adhesive fabric described on page 75, or contact the manufacturers for their advice.

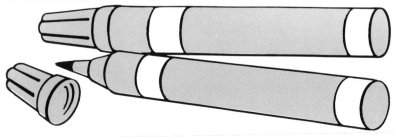

Magnetic boards

Either wet-wipe or dry-wipe surfacing materials can be mounted on to a metal core to make a magnet board.

THE MAGNETS ARE IN THE ACCESSORIES, NOT THE BOARD

There is a wide variety of ready-made magnetic symbols, letters, numbers, tapes and discs available for charting, critical-flow paths, graphs and so forth.

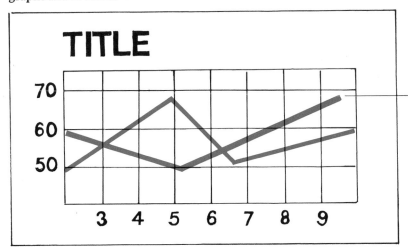

Magnetic tapes can be placed in position before, or during the presentation

For DIY enthusiasts, there are brightly coloured magnetic tiles which can be cut to any shape with a sharp knife or scissors. Mark the required shape on to the front of the tile in pencil and cut along the guidelines.

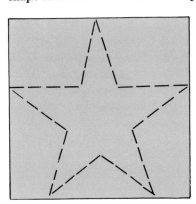
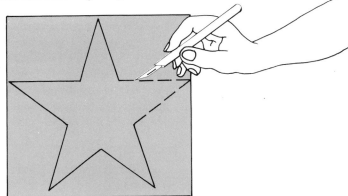

If the shape is complicated, make a paper pattern and transfer this to the tile and cut, using a stout knife or scissors, or place paper over the tile and cut tile and paper together.

Cutting complicated shapes
1. Make paper pattern of shape.
2. Place pattern over tile or card, tape in position.
3. Go over outlines firmly with a ball-point pen.
4. Remove pattern and go over the imprint in ink, or cut along the grooves if no outline is needed.

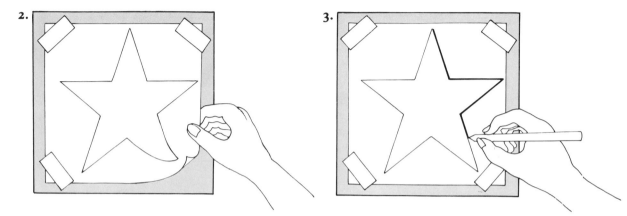

If you work out the shape on the back of the card or tile (to avoid marking the front) you may need to work in reverse.

If you draw the pattern on thin paper you will only have to turn it over to get a mirror image.

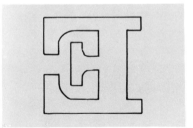

Self-adhesive magnetic tape. This kind of tape can be attached to photos, empty boxes (your latest product), DIY symbols, banners – in fact, to almost anything you want to display. The amount of tape needed to hold the article firmly in position will depend on its weight.

If you are making the aids at home, attach them to the side of the fridge for an hour or so to check whether they slide down or fall off the surface. If they do, add more tape.

Banners are coloured boxes (white does not stand out on white) containing the key points and other information requiring emphasis. Less important or variable data can be written directly on to the board close to the relevant caption.

The presenter can add the banners as and when they are required to build up the theme, and this method of displaying the information is useful when presenting statistics; see page 80.

DIY banners

Equipment needed:
- Self-adhesive magnetic tape
- Coloured card or paper
- Cardboard for backing (cereal boxes and other cartons)
- Broad-tipped markers
- Scissors or knife
- Pencil and rule
- Stapler or paper adhesive

The minimum banner width is approximately 76 mm (3 inches) displaying 50 mm (2 inch) letters with a 13 mm (½ inch) border on either side.

1. Rule the banner divisions (at least 3 inches (76 mm) wide) on to the coloured paper or card.
2. Lightly rule in the lettering guides.

2″ Lettering Guide

3″ Banner

3. Stick the paper to the card with paper gum or staples.
4. Cut carefully along the dividing lines, using scissors or knife and straight edge.
5. Roughly letter the captions, in pencil.
6. Neatly ink over, using a colour that contrasts with the background.

7. Attach magnetic strip to the back. 25 mm (1 inch) either end of a 30 cm (12 inch) strip is sufficient; longer banners may need one in the middle. There is no hard-and-fast rule about the length of banners but they should be easy to handle and a long caption can be divided into sections.
8. Add the number of the banner to back, session title and any lecture notes that are needed as a reminder. You can quickly glance at the notes before putting the banner on the board – it saves using a script.
9. Store file banners in envelopes or polythene bags. Do not use rubber bands as these can dent a lightweight card.

Building up information

Bar graphs can be built up using blocks of colour on an inked base. The base lines can be drawn in a spirit-based ink if you are worried about accidentally removing it when you add the bars (the special cleaning fluid must be used to erase this or you will damage the board surface).

The build-up technique is also useful for showing the stages in a process or displaying step-by-step instructions.

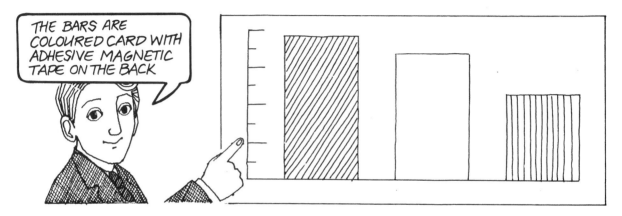

Ad libbing. Keep a few blank banners ready in case you need quickly to add a point during the presentation. Provided that the guidelines have been ruled in beforehand, it will not take a minute to write in the few words needed.

Summary

10. Ad libbing with aids

Any unprepared notes and diagrams that are introduced during the presentation still need to be kept brief and to the point.

This is not too much of a problem when the aid is being used to emphasize or explain a point raised by the presenter, but it can go awry when used to show information being fed back by the audience, as in a discussion group or review session.

When the comments are coming at you fast and furious, the temptation is to scrawl quickly and verbatim whatever has been said.

The art is to:
1. Remain in control – take the comments one at a time and in your own time.
2. Avoid writing while you are listening.
3. Summarize the comments, extract the key points.
4. Precisely and legibly write these points on the aid.
5. Cross through any mistake you might make firmly, or erase it and add the correction.
6. Stand clear of the aid while assessing the next comment.

Using the film roll (Overhead Projector)
If you have trouble keeping your writing straight, use a ruled sheet of film underneath the roll as a guide. This sheet will need to be removed when the film roll is wound on.

The ruled films are available with handwriting guides, music staves and squares.

Making additions while you talk
If you prefer not to mark the transparency when you make additions or emphasize points, slip it underneath the film roll and write on that instead.

Emphasizing information

Draw the main part of the transparency in permanent ink, leaving the spaces for the points you want to highlight. The blanks can be filled in during the presentation with water-soluble ink which can be erased later without damaging the base information.

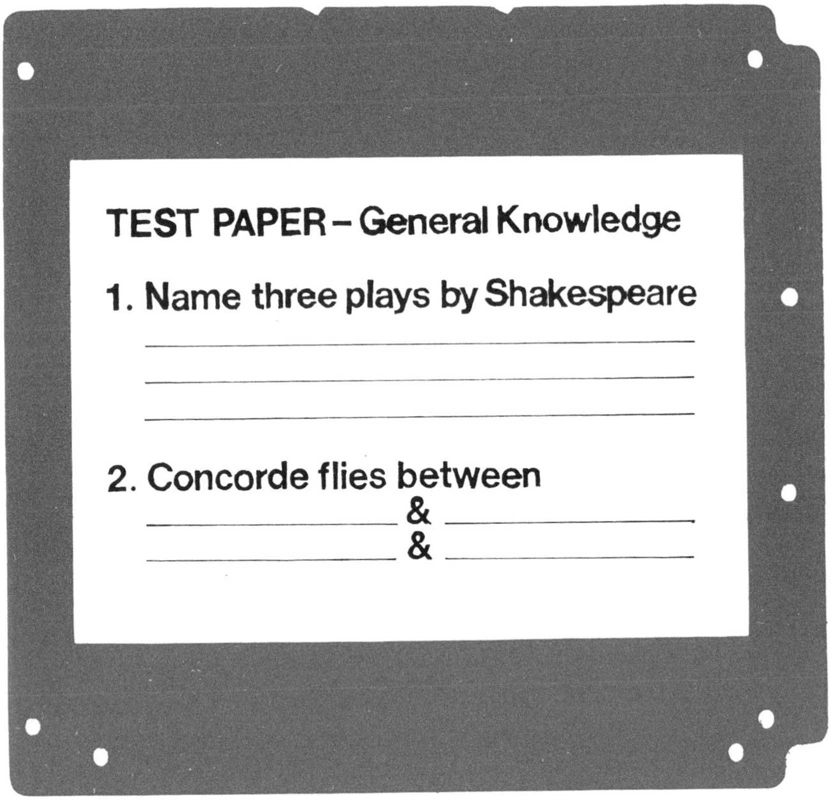

TEST PAPER – General Knowledge

1. Name three plays by Shakespeare

_____

_____

_____

2. Concorde flies between

_____ & _____

_____ & _____

Summary
Avoid taking
Dictation
List
Important points
Briefly

II. Presenting statistics

Many people, myself included, have enough difficulty with their multiplication tables, let alone with the perplexing task of trying to fathom out and remember long lists of figures flashed briefly on to a screen.

The A B C of presenting statistics

Bear in mind the essentials of a good visual; page 17.

Accuracy, brevity and clarity and extend the formula to include:
Analyse
Breakdown
Camouflage

Analyse: Select and mark up the facts that must be seen. Ignore what might be useful in case you forget to mention it or someone asks an awkward question. You can always refer to your sheet of figures when you talk — nobody will expect you to remember the lot. Or you can issue the audience with comprehensive handouts; some will read them, some will not, but none of them will be able to read the overcrowded visuals anyway.

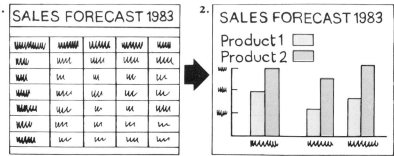

1. Suitable as a handout but not as a visual.
2. Contains the essential points taken from 1 and is far easier to read and remember.

Visual comment: bar charts (histograms) are useful for showing comparisons as they save the viewer the bother of mentally comparing the difference between quantities.

Breakdown: Separate complex information into sections and use one visual per section or use one of the display techniques described on page 61 to present a maze of facts in easy-to-comprehend stages.

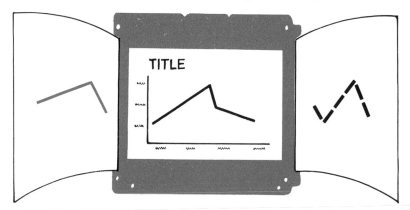

Camouflage: No, not to disguise the facts, but to make a dry topic more acceptable by using visually interesting introductory and summarizing visuals to lift the presentation.

For example: a sales or marketing session could be introduced with a cartoon lion cued in with, 'Who'll get the lion's share of the market in 1983?' And next year the title and product will be the only alterations needed to update the visual, so making it a useful time-saver too.

The reasoning behind this is simple. The introduction should attract the audience's attention and make them think, 'This looks interesting.' The summary should send them away thinking, 'That was interesting. I think I'll read the handout.' If you intend talking for any length of time, you will also need a few reasonable visuals between the statistics.

Making the most of what's available

If you are short of time and have to make visuals directly from a typed sheet, make sure that:

1. The letter height is at least 6 mm (¼ inch) and lines are double spaced.
2. A background colour film is used to cut down the glare and make the printed information stand out.
3. If you have time, add colour bands to emphasize the main points or ring them if they are scattered about the sheet. Also, colour can be overlayed to allow a step-by-step build-up of the facts.

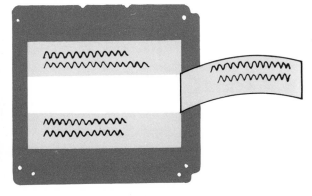

Reverse image visuals. Another way to improve the readability of small letters is to use a reverse-image film; the highlighting can be done with OHP pens or strips of colour film.

Printed grids. There is a variety of printed grids available which can save the time and bother of drawing outlines and measuring scales. If none of these fit your requirements, draw a set of your own, photocopy, and file for future use.

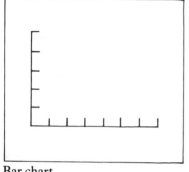

Bar chart

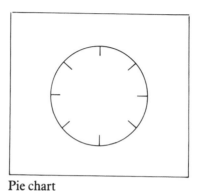

Pie chart

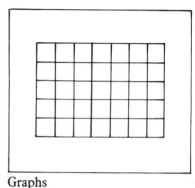

Graphs

The graph or squared paper rough is invaluable if no other grid is to hand.

Graphs are one of the simplest ways pictorially to present figures, and they can be improved by the use of colour, as the diagrams show. Neither the horizontal nor the vertical scales need to start at 0; if all the data is over 2,000, start at 2,000 to save space. Scales need to be identified, but avoid writing the vertical scale title from top to bottom since it will make it more difficult to read.

Use thick, coloured graph lines; again, these can be overlayed if necessary.

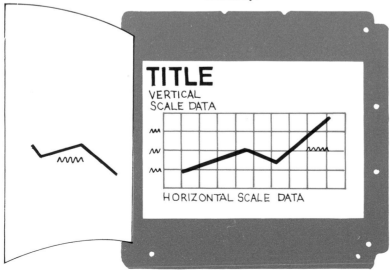

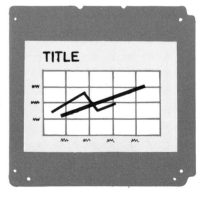

A coloured border makes the central data area stand out

Reverse image graphs can be 'animated' by placing opaque sticking tape over the lines and peeling it off to make the lines 'grow'.

Bar charts (histograms) are useful for showing the state of affairs at a given point. Colour and overlays can be used to separate the information, and scale data and base-line data should be marked. If the bars are divided, numerical information should be included since it can be difficult for the audience to assess the amounts quickly.

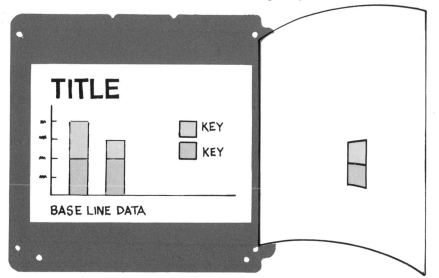

The bars can also run across the visual. I am sure most of you have seen charts with lines of symbols representing amounts. Drawing these takes time, and they are not usually on view for long enough to justify the extra work. And beware of converting the upright bars to symbols, because someone who is half asleep might just think that the heights are relative to the social status (another distractor, see page 91).

Pie charts. The precise division of circles requires a protractor, but for visuals there is no need to be that accurate so long as the numerical data is indicated in or near each section.

The easiest way to divide the 'pie' is with a straight edge and pencil – ½=50 per cent, ¼=25 per cent, ⅛=12½ per cent, 1/16=6¼ per cent and so on. Thus approximately 20 per cent is obtained by adding ⅛ to 1/16 of the circle.

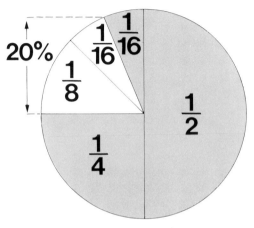

Colour should be added to highlight main points (see page 43), but avoid using strong shades on unimportant sections.

And, of course, overlays will help to emphasize the sections.

MAKE THE IMPORTANT POINTS VISUALLY DOMINANT.

Filling in forms

This can create quite a problem, especially when the form cannot be cut in any way and the space on the transparency is too small for the presenter to write in easily and legibly as he or she talks. There are two ways to handle this:

1. Project the form on to a whiteboard and fill in the information on the board where the projected linespacing will be wider.
2. Write the additional information on to strips of film and overlay each point separately. To make the additions stand out, either write in a different colour ink or add colour to the strips.

Charting techniques for boards and flipcharts

The basic diagram and chart outlines are the same as for OHP, but the 'build-up' techniques are different.

'Ghosting'. Instead of using overlays, the presenter can build up the information by adding it to a prepared base during the presentation. The additions can be 'ghosted' on to the sheet or board lightly in pencil and inked over when required. Try to use the most vibrant colours for the extra data, and do not forget to rule lettering guidelines for identifying notes.

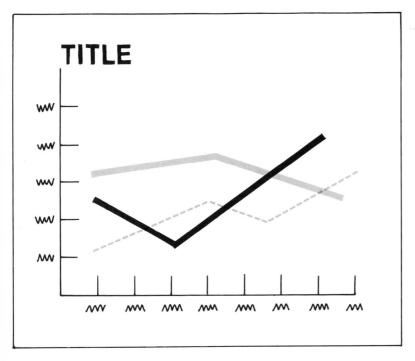

Charting on boards. For charts which need regular updates or alterations, draw the base outlines, notes and so forth in a permanent ink and add the variable information in a non-permanent ink so that the base will remain intact when the corrections are made; see page 76.

Summary

12. Distractors

Distractors divert the attention of the audience away from the message, some obscure it completely.

Distractors can:
- Reduce comprehension of subject-matter.
- Complicate the task of conveying the information.
- Increase the time needed to convey the information.

Most speakers develop their own way of handling garrulous members of the audience and hecklers. Such distractions are difficult to anticipate, and have to be dealt with as and when they occur, but there are attention-losers which can, with forethought, be avoided.

Visual comment: Well-known symbols are quickly and easily recognized and can be used to reinforce the message.

The usual distractions are caused by one or more of the following:
- The presenter
- The pictures (visuals)
- The place

Many of the pitfalls have already been mentioned, so I shall simply list the relevant pages for your reference.

Remember the rules for a good visual:

A GOOD VISUAL IS:
- BIG and BOLD
- CLEAR and CONCISE
- STIMULATES INTEREST
- ATTRACTS ATTENTION
- GETS THE MESSAGE ACROSS

The place. The problem of finding and booking a suitable room rarely arises in schools, colleges or training centres but for those who have to find a suitable venue, here are the points to watch:
- The position and size of the room
- Internal/external noise

Position
1. Try to make it easily accessible for the audience. They might be disinclined to trek cross-country to attend.
2. Make sure your room is not *en route* for another office, or it could become like working in a corridor, and there is nothing quite so distracting as Mabel and Flo trundling through with the tea trolley.

Size: check that it will take you, your aids (with enough distance between projector and screen), your equipment and the audience *in comfort*.

Internal noise: the worst offenders are telephones and intercoms, so veto all calls and turn off the tannoy. The switchboard operator and secretaries can take messages or tell callers when to ring back.

External noise: try to avoid rooms by the main road or any other noisy thoroughfare or you could find yourself competing for the audience's attention with a couple of road drills, or the rush-hour traffic.

Summary

In order to communicate effectively to a group of people, it is important to stop their attention from wandering or being diverted away from the message.

Distractors to avoid

Disturbances:
Illegible or indistinct visuals
Speakers who mumble or
Talk to their Aids.
Redundant or
Ambiguous information
Careless ad libs
Timekeeping
Internal/external noise
Other visuals
Non-stop funnies
Sidetracking from the main point

13. Presentation format

- INTRODUCTION
- CONTENTS
- SUMMARY
- CLOSE

Whether the presentation is a single half-hour chat or part of a course, at the beginning the audience will want to know:

1. Why the speaker is there.
2. Why they are there.
3. What to expect.

Certain aspects of a regular session, such as timing, become routine, but introductions are still necessary for:

1. New topics.
2. Guest speakers.
3. Variations from the norm.

Introduction

The initial introduction should include the following points:

WHO — The speaker. The audience won't need a *curriculum vitae*, just enough to convince them that he or she is worth listening to.

WHAT — The topic and objective of the presentation.

WHY — They should attend, i.e. what's in it for them?

HOW — The information is to be given. Will it be a lecture, a demonstration, a film show, a discussion or practical session, and *will they be expected to participate?*

WHEN — To ask questions – at the end?
— as and when they occur?
Timing – coffee and lunch breaks.
the end of the session.

WHERE— To obtain equipment, reports. Whether to take notes or if supporting handouts are to be made available.

The content

The information should be presented systematically with a logical follow-through between points.

If you go off at a tangent, don't assume that the audience can or will keep up with you. You are familiar with your subject, but your talk may be the first they have heard of it.

And it will not be simply a case of regaining their attention. You may have to regain their interest as well.

So, present the SEQUENCE logically

STRESS the key points visually and verbally

SUMMARIZE before moving on to a new topic or idea

SUPPORT your claims with examples, illustration, demonstrations

IF YOU CONFUSE 'EM
YOU'LL LOSE 'EM!

The summary

Before you close:

1. Give a brief résumé of your ideas and recap the key points.
   This will – Reinforce the key points.
               – Make sure that you have not forgotten anything.
               – Help those who may have missed something.
2. Remind the audience to take handouts, reports, etc.

Close

Tell them:

1. When and if you will be back, and the topic of the next talk.
2. Remove all of your aids, notes and special effects.

Summary

14. Presentation techniques

Every presenter develops their own style and way of getting the message across. Many of us rely on our personalities, voices or our own particular 'brand of magic' to gain and hold attention, particularly when the topic is dry or the audience cold.

Many of these skills are acquired with practice, experience and constant objective assessment of an audience's reaction to our efforts. As far as I am concerned, a good presentation manner is obtained as much by applying common sense as by applying psychology. So, for those who are new to the game, here are some ways to make sure that your sessions run smoothly, leaving you with an audience who would not object to attending your next performance.

Presentation checklist

Before the presentation:

1. **Practise using the visuals,** especially if you are using animation or display techniques. Plan banner layouts on whiteboards.
2. **Check the timing.** Plan to run to time (record the chat and adjust if necessary). If you over-run the audience may become fidgety and the next presenter may have to cut short their talk to keep to the timetable.
3. **Organize equipment.** Either take your own or advise those responsible of your needs. If you are a visiting speaker, check what is available before deciding which aids to use.
4. **Check and set equipment.** Put visuals and notes in order of presentation.

Giving the presentation:

1. **Be punctual.**
2. **Avoid distractors such as:**
   (a) Obviously looking at your watch while you talk. Either place it on the desk where you can see it easily or wear it with the face on the inside of the wrist so that you can discreetly check the time.
   (b) Pacing to and fro while you talk, especially if your route takes you in front of your visual aids. Pacing presenters not only risk irritating the audience, but, as they move, the direction of their voice alters and those who are behind the presenter sometimes miss what is being said.
   (c) Any mannerisms that take the audience's attention away from the message you are trying to convey. There is no need to stand to attention, but if you wave your arms about too much you will draw their eyes away from your visuals.
   (d) Blocking the view.
3. **Avoid staring** continually at one section or individual in the audience. It is most disconcerting to be the object of such attention, and the rest of the group will feel excluded.
   Talk to them all.
   Look at them all, and keep your eyes moving to pick up the feedback.

Do:

1. **Appear to be enthusiastic** about your subject. If you seem bored it will be transferred to the audience.
2. **Give them time to see and read** the visuals before you move on to the next item.
3. **Remove unwanted aids from view.** Flip over charts, clean boards, turn off projectors (see page 15 for correct projection procedure).
4. **Speak clearly,** do not mumble. If you need to refer to your notes, do not look down while you read because your voice will be directed to the floor not the audience, and those at the back might miss the chat.

   Pause – rather than 'um and ah'.
   – to allow the point to sink in.
   – to emphasize a point.

   Pitch your voice level so that everyone can hear you.
   – vary pitch to stress a point.

   Pace – vary pace of speech to avoid monotony.
   to emphasize a point.

   Reinforce important points by repeating them.
5. **Smile.**

> YOU ARE YOUR OWN VISUAL AID AND EVEN THE MOST HARD-NOSED AUDIENCE EVENTUALLY RESPONDS TO A PLEASANT PRESENTER WHO LOOKS PLEASED TO BE THERE

After the presentation. Make a note of the questions asked and, if necessary, adjust the presentation accordingly.

Summary

If you find it a lot to remember along with all the information that you are trying to convey, take it one step at a time and, whatever else you do:

SPEAK UP
DON'T STARE
STAND CLEAR OF THE AIDS
ENTHUSE
AND KEEP SMILING

SOFTWARE INDEX – OHP

Product	How to use	Details	Comments	Available from	
				Artshops	AV suppliers
Film Clear	pages 23, 26, 61	Size – 10″×8″, 10″×10″, A4, sheets or pads	Write or draw on directly using OHP pens	●	●
Direct copy	page 23	A4	Write, draw or type		●
Coloured	page 44	Size – 10″×10″, A4, sheets. Colours – red, orange, yellow, green, blue, pink	Darker colours available, but do not project well	●	●
Film Rolls	pages 7, 81	Size – various, depends on OHP	Not all OHPs have film-roll attachments		●
Coloured self-adhesive projection film	page 45	Size – usually A4. Colours – red, orange, yellow, green, blue, brown and grey	Special non-projectible adhesive used. Ordinary coloured adhesive film not suitable	●	●
Printed film sheets	page 58	Size – A4	Handwriting guide squares, music staves		●
Animation film	page 66	Motions, flows, turbulence, spinning	2 types available, equipment not interchangeable		●
Copying film – Thermal	page 48	Size – 10″×8½″, A4. Type – black line on clear; black line on colour; colour line on clear; reversal	Use with thermal, copier. Not light-sensitive. Fast, clean process		●
Diazo film	page 53	Black line on clear; black line on colour; colour on clear; reversal	Longer process than thermal, but good reproduction. Film is light-sensitive		●
Paper copier film	page 55	Black line on clear and colour			●
Markers – water soluble & permanent	pages 22, 40	Colours as OHP pens		●	●

Product	How to use	Details	Comments	Available from	
				Artshops	AV suppliers
Pens – water soluble and permanent	pages 8, 22, 40	Colours – black, red, green, blue, brown, yellow, orange, purple	*Important:* Recap immediately after use. Do not use blade to remove inks from film – the scratch marks will project	●	●
Pencils	page 22	Colours – black, red, blue, green	Water soluble only		●
Technical pens – water soluble & permanent	page 22	Line width – fine, medium, broad Colours – black, red, blue, green	Can be used for stencilling directly onto film as well as drawing		●
Eraser – OHP Rubbers, cleaning fluids and cleaning tissues and pens	page 22	Will remove permanent inks without damaging film			●
Compass		Has special foot which will not mark the film	Takes OHP pens and can be used on film or paper		●
Lettering – Thermal letters	pages 31, 32	Heat resistant. Letters and numbers in various sizes and styles	Special dry transfer lettering. Use on paper and pass through copier		●
Projection Letters	pages 27, 28	Various sizes and styles in red, black, green, blue, yellow	Apply directly to film	●	●
Frames	page 59	Aperture = 10″×8″, 10″×10″, A4			●
Pointer	page 16	Telescopic or clear perspex			●
Ring Binders/ Carrying Case	page 60	For storage	L.P. Record cases also suitable		●
Clip Art Books	page 41	Loose leaf & hard back available.	No copyright applies		●

Lettering guide for approx. 20′ viewing distance (screen to backrow)

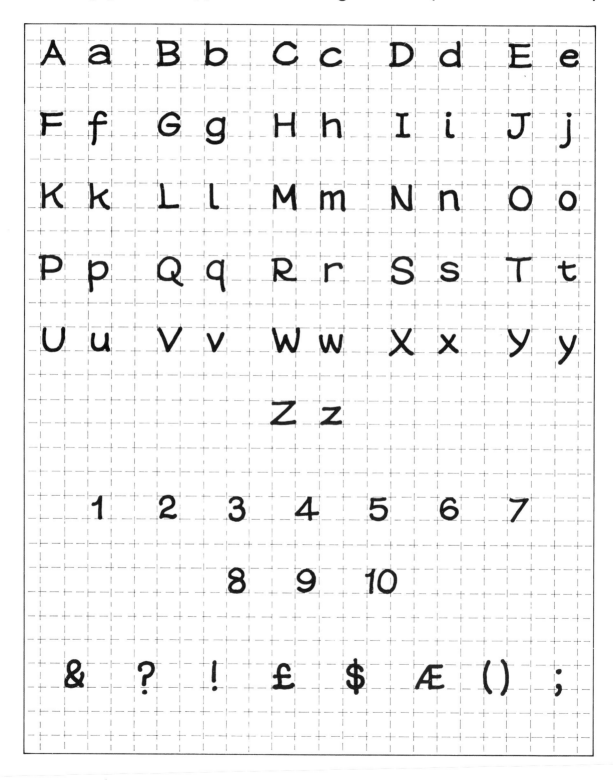

Lettering guide for approx. 30′ viewing distance (screen to backrow)

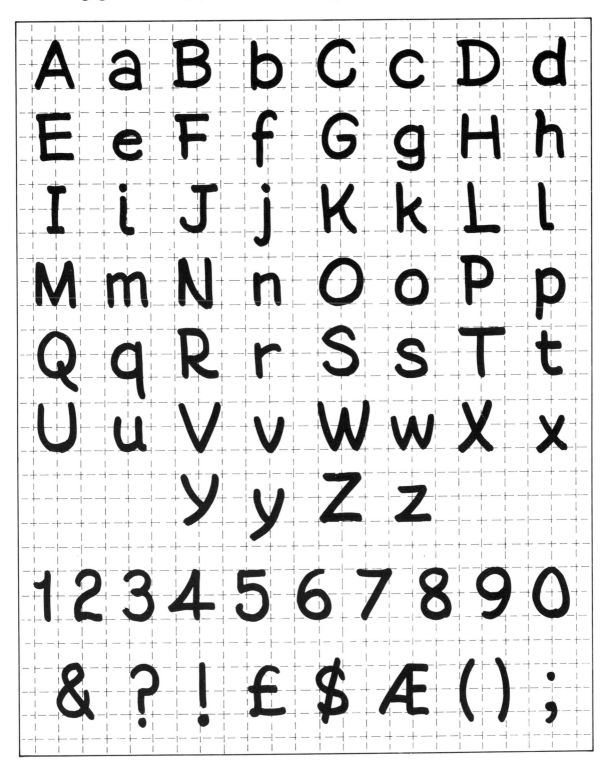

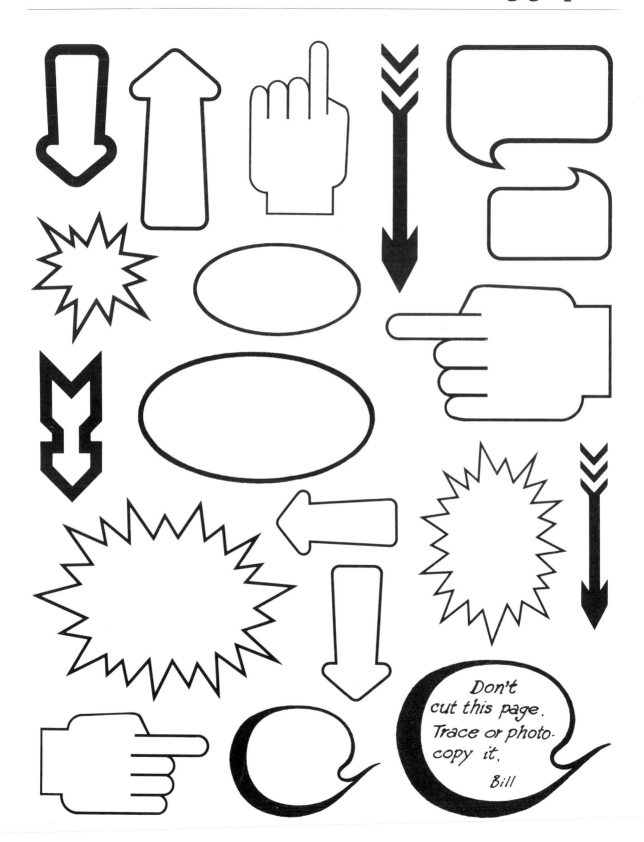

Index

Resources Centre

Centre for Teaching,
Learning & Assessment

The University of

www.tla.ed.ac.uk